75 YEARS OF THE TIMES CROSSWORD

TIMES BOOKS

FOREWORD

Colin Dexter

I feel honoured in being asked to pull together the fictional world of Inspector Morse – with his passion for *The Times* Crossword – and the genuine affection that countless others, including me, feel for these puzzles.

Like the Greenwich pips and the British pubs, *The Times* Crossword is a national institution, with the ability to solve it recognized as a benchmark of mental acumen and flexibility. All addicts are reasonably familiar with being asked how long it takes them to complete, and answers (where honest) vary enormously – from the under four minutes of Roy Dean, authenticated by *The Guinness Book of Records*, to Milton's timing of Satan's fall from heaven – 'from morn to noon, from noon to dewy eve'. I'm somewhere in the middle myself; but even after more than five decades of practice I not infrequently find myself infuriated at being unable to solve that one final clue. Morse could almost invariably complete the puzzle at supersonic speed; and 'Not now, Lewis!' was a common enough reprimand when his sergeant found the courage to interrupt him with some vital information on the latest murder. Once, to be fair to him, Morse did try to interest Lewis in the clue *'Take in bachelor? This could well do (3)'.* But without success.

What is its degree of difficulty? In the 'fiendish' category we have the former *Listener* puzzles, blessedly salvaged by *The Times* and printed each Saturday in the *Books* section. I will not dwell on it, since I usually have inordinate difficulty in understanding the rubric, let alone solving the puzzle. At the bottom of the range is the simple (!) definition-only coffee-break variety. This sort of thing: 1 ac. *'River (3)'*; 1 dn *'Fish (3)'*. Well CAM/COD; DEE/DAB; EXE/EEL, etc. Who knows? And who cares? *The Times* maintains its traditional position in the upper-middle category, with the firm dedication of its setters to 'fair play', that is, saying what they mean in however oblique, misleading, but grammatically – and syntactically – correct formulation, always telling solvers what is to be done with words and letters, etc. For me such a faith in setters is of paramount importance, since for ninety-nine per cent of the time I know they will 'play fair' with me; and therefore my greatest delight results from a struggle when the penny finally drops and suddenly the answer is simple and obvious – quite often memorable, too. It is in this last respect that such fine number-puzzles as Su Doku must ever sadly pale in comparison with the lure of the crossword, since their final impersonal answers are inevitably unmemorable – and indeed unmemorizable.

Recollection of favourite clues from the daily challenge is much more like greeting old friends anew, and even after many years such clues are so easily memorized. I once wrote to *The Times* Crossword to say that I considered the following clue the finest offering of the previous two decades: *'For whom right and wrong can go in ledger (9, 5)'*. Later I learned that Brian Greer was its author, and (pleasingly) that he has kept my letter. Fairly recently Mike Laws reminded us of the wonderful four-fold word-play in *'They tend to bring up unrelated issues (6, 7)'*. I could go on and on … Incidentally, a third former editor, John Grant, was the only person I ever met who had successfully spotted the clues to be found in the Morse novels which gave away the Chief Inspector's first name.

A great, and I think, unique tribute for me personally was to have *The Times* Crossword headed 'Morse – Whodunnit', in which members of the Morse team were to be found cleverly concealed in

CONTENTS

THE TIMES

75 YEARS OF THE TIMES CROSSWORD

TIMES BOOKS

Published in 2005 by Times Books

This edition produced for
The Book People Ltd
Hall Wood Avenue
Haydock St Helens WA11 9UL

www.harpercollins.co.uk
Visit the booklover's website

ISBN: 0–00–777349–8

British Library Cataloguing in Publication Date
A catalogue record for this book is available from the British Library.

Special acknowledgement to David Akenhead for proof editing
Designed and typeset by White-Card, London
Printed and bound in Great Britain by Clays Ltd, St Ives plc

the completed grid. And as I look again at that particular puzzle I find a clue which for me epitomizes some of the key qualities I most admire: '*Queen's favourite cheese (9)*'—with its brevity, humour, deceptive wording, and the need for that bit of general knowledge.

Not that our crossword is without its faults, and I mention three minor grouses of my own. First, why this coy persistence with the anonymity of our setters? Almost all of us would be interested in their identities – or at least the names they've given themselves. Second, why not stick the puzzle where it belongs – on the back page? I felt much sympathy with one of the letters to the Editor protesting that he had never previously practised the skills of origami, and had no further wish to do so. Third, why not, occasionally, re-introduce the old-fashioned feature of printing a line of poetry with the clue's answer omitted from it? Such clues give a sense of smug superiority (and an easy start!) to those familiar with the poem in question; and the opportunity for those who aren't to do some research in the collected works and to find not only the relevant line but also many other wholly irrelevant delights into the bargain.

In sum, solving a crossword is for me the most civilized and enjoyable way I've yet discovered (though I'm only seventy-five) of wasting countless hours of my leisure time. In this foreword I have tried to suggest some of the reasons why this is so, and why Inspector Morse and myself became such devoted addicts of *The Times* Crossword.

Answers to clues:
Take in bachelor, this could well do (3) – BRA
For whom right and wrong can go in ledger (9,5) – RECORDING ANGEL
They tend to bring up unrelated issues (6,7) – FOSTER PARENTS
Queen's favourite cheese (9) – LEICESTER

MORSE – WHODUNNIT

18 March 1993

Across

1. Keeping out of French local association (9)
6. Artistic circle's quarrel about name (5)
9. Turn left in female chorus's first movement (7)
10. Was idle and wanted out of university (7)
11. Person going up for part of flight (5)
12. Queen's favourite cheese (9)
13. Broadcast is essentially produced by head of drama (8)
15. Constable, for example, as portrait painter (4)
19. Become more friendly—what's new? (4)
20. Administrative head taking over northern section (8)
23. Ruin of e.g. Eric at start of teens? (9)
24. Deposit old coin in box (5)
26. State in which pages are bound to appear (7)
27. Mark time in descent (7)
28. Surrendered with good chance of winning, say (5)
29. Former treatment of rioters? They're shot outside (9)

Down

1. Refuse to buy ruddy Italian record, initially (9)
2. Writer of poetry similar to Brooke's, say (5)
3. King with sword conceals cunning riposte (8)
4. Visionary thought to be unbalanced (8)
5. Person who can help fisherman to catch with net, that is (6)
6. Transport—true or false? (6)
7. It's put on late, near midnight in London (5–4)
8. Instruct a class (5)
14. Surprised it's not synchronized (9)
16. Never composed? Not so! (9)
17. Insurance grant that's topping for retired person (8)
18. Carriage monarch provided for European citizen (8)
21. Supported people replacing characters within board (6)
22. The party that's in (2-4)
23. Firm master in charge raising a laugh (5)
25. Party introduces right bill for law and order extremist (5)

Cachet Associated with Doing The Times Crossword

Ability to do *The Times* Crossword is widely regarded as an indicator of erudition and intelligence. In *The Wench is Dead,* this is how Inspector Morse begins a journey from Oxford: *He bought* The Times *and* The Oxford Times *at the bookstall, got a seat at the rear of the train and had solved* The Times *Crossword by Didcot. Except for one clue … He quickly wrote in a couple of bogus letters (in case any of his fellow-passengers were waiting to be impressed).*

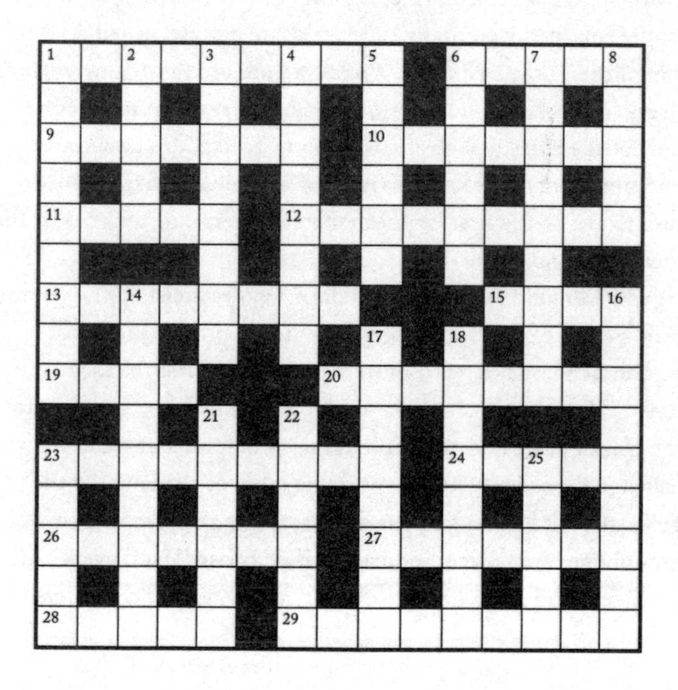

INTRODUCTION

The Times came a little late to the crossword party – our serial number will for ever be behind those of the *Guardian* and *Daily Telegraph* – but our reputation quickly made up for our junior status. What was it about those early puzzles that established us as the classic of our type? I think it was our particular combination of difficulty and erudition: the puzzles required a wide and deep range of cultural knowledge, suited to our readership of those days which typically graduated from governess to public school to Oxford and Cambridge; and the clues themselves were more allusive than specific, in particular giving little of the helpful wordplay we are used to today, so that solvers had to bear a number of possible answers in mind for many of the clues, which made it more crucial to know the quotations and other specific tests of knowledge that enabled them to put in the first cross-checking letters and thus begin the process of elimination.

It was Edmund Akenhead as editor who established the features we now expect of the modern puzzle: more precise and fairer construction of clues, with more wordplay and less reliance on mere recall of dusty school lessons. Today, a nodding acquaintance with Shakespeare and the Bible remains helpful, but we also may challenge the solver with the periodic table of elements, or the names of Walt Disney's seven dwarfs; but our anagrams and homophones are now all indicated (if deviously!), and every clue contains a scrupulous definition. But, as always, our compilers continue to strive to create those perfect clues, a feature of our crossword down the years, whose apparently effortless surface sense leads the solver teasingly but quite properly in entirely the wrong direction.

I would like to record my thanks to those many people who have contributed to this book: particularly to my predecessor John Grant, whose archives were a mine of material, to Polly Tatum (née Carton) and Anthea Bell for their recollections of earlier days, to Paul King at *The Times* library, to Mark Holland at the Gales archive, to David Akenhead for proof editing, and to the many readers who wrote in with memories and anecdotes. *The Times* Crossword, however exasperating it may occasionally prove, clearly retains widespread affection, and long may it thrive.

Richard Browne
Editor of *The Times* Crossword

THE CULT OF THE CROSSWORD

What is the world's favourite intellectual pastime – is it chess, bridge, mah jongg, backgammon, Scrabble? No, it's none of these – it's solving crossword puzzles.

The crossword puzzle is one of the most universally popular inventions of the twentieth century. In Britain alone, several million people enjoy their daily dose of puzzling. It's estimated that over 80 per cent of the world's daily newspapers carry some form of crossword, as well as many weekly newspapers and magazines.

The crossword appears to be a combination of the old acrostics and word squares which date back to ancient Greece. The first one was devised in 1913 by Arthur Wynne, an English journalist working on the *New York Sunday World*. Looking to provide his readers with some entertainment, he composed a diamond-shaped grid with all the words interlocking and simple definition clues. He called it a 'Word-cross'.

But it wasn't until April 1924, with the publication of the first crossword puzzle book, that the craze took off. It immediately swept America and dominated social life. It got so bad that dictionaries had to be provided on trains so that commuters could do their puzzles.

A scornful editorial in *The Times* in December 1924 noted that 'All America had succumbed to the crossword puzzle ... The crossword is a menace because it is making devastating inroads on the working hours of every rank of society'. But two months later *The Times* had to admit that the craze had crossed the Atlantic with 'the speed of a meteorological depression'.

The Times itself held out as long as it could, but in the end it bowed to public pressure and published its first crossword on 1st February 1930. It was one of the first daily papers to move away from the simple definition type of clue and introduce the 'cryptic' puzzle in which each clue is a kind of riddle which has to be unravelled before the solver can arrive at the answer. Its diamond jubilee in 1990 was marked with great celebrations and worldwide coverage.

Though not the most difficult of its kind, its consistent qualities of sophisticated wordplay and sly humour have won it a reputation as the most famous crossword in the world. It frequently features in novels, plays and films where the author wished to establish a character of high intelligence. The annual *Times* National Crossword Championship, which began in 1970, attracted up to 30,000 entrants, and the final became a most exciting event as the keenest minds in the country worked through four puzzles against the clock.

Why should the cryptic crossword have developed only in Britain? One answer is the Englishman's fondness for wordplay. The 1920s were a period when the country house party was at its height, and it was customary for people to settle down to charades and pencil-and-paper games after dinner. Edward Powys Mathers, a critic, poet, and translator, picked up this tradition and translated it into the crossword, calling himself Torquemada after the Grand Inquisitor.

Secondly, the English language has evolved over time as a melting-pot of words derived from many sources. In addition to the Romance and North European languages which form the basis of the English tongue, there are words brought back by Britons from the former colonies, infusions from Chinese and Russian, contributions from Turkish and Arabic. Greek provides the basis of political thought, science and technology, Latin for religion, medicine and the arts.

English has eagerly taken in everything. Consequently, the language contains many words with multiple meanings, deriving from completely different roots. Even short words like 'set' can have a hundred different meanings. And it is not uncommon for a single word like 'round' to serve as noun, verb, adverb, adjective and preposition. These ambiguities are seized upon by crafty crossword compilers who manipulate the language to their own ends to mislead the solver.

Thirdly, the English language is unique in possessing so many short words which can be used to make up longer ones to which they are in no way related. Take the word 'insignificant' for example. It breaks down neatly into 'in-sign-if-I-can't'. Or 'refrigerator', which becomes 'ref-rig-era-tor'. Tricks of this kind are the meat and drink of crossword compilers. With the most sophisticated practitioners of this form of literary fun, 'brainwash' may be broken down as 'bra-in-wash' and clued as 'Bust down reason'.

Anagrams are no longer indicated by the symbol 'anag.' in brackets but by words in the clue suggesting confusion, error, drunkenness, building, possibility, and so on. Thus, 'The President saw nothing wrong' may be construed as 'Washington'. Taking this to its highest form, the whole clue becomes a definition of the answer, as in 'Thing called shaky illumination?', giving 'candlelight'.

Then there are many instances of one word slipped inside another to make a third, as in 'ca(bare)t', 'come(lines)s' and 'th(ink)ing'. Sometimes a word is hidden; for example, 'Prime Minister seen in the Athenaeum' gives 'Heath'.

Another popular device is words that sound alike: 'wether', 'weather'and 'whether' are typical of this kind. In some cases a foreign import can sound like an English word: the rubber substance 'gutta-percha' becomes the street urchin 'gutter-percher'. The crossword compiler has all these tricks up his sleeve, and many more. His tool is to use the English in its infinite flexibility, and he uses it to baffle the solver in a devious but entertaining fashion. So there is always a feeling of enormous satisfaction as you enter the final solution in a *Times* Crossword.

Roy Dean – twice winner of *The Times* Crossword Championship, 1970 and 1979, and world record holder since 1970 for the fastest verified solution of *The Times* Crossword.

PUBLIC REACTION TO THE TIMES CROSSWORD IN 1930

Thursday, January 16, 1930

Sir, —I am interested to see that you are including a cross-word puzzle in your Weekly Edition. Would it not be an additional attraction to your many readers – of whom I am pleased to be one – if the same cross-word puzzle were reproduced on one day of the week in your daily edition? Perhaps you could find space in your columns to publish this letter, and thus ascertain the opinions of my fellow-readers.

Saturday, January 18, 1930

Many correspondents have written in response to the suggestion, made in a letter last Thursday, that The Times *should reproduce in one of its daily issues the cross-word puzzles published in its Weekly Edition. A few of the comments on the proposal are printed below:*

Sir, —We are two regular readers of *The Times* and cordially endorse Lieutenant-Commander Powell's suggestion to insert a crossword puzzle in your daily edition.

Sir, —I hope that there will be a sufficient response to Commander Powell's letter asking for a weekly crossword in your daily edition to encourage you to carry out his suggestion.

Sir, —As one who values *The Times* more than any other newspaper I should like to support the plea of Lieutenant-Commander A. C. Powell for at least an occasional crossword puzzle. I do so because in my household the desire for one was long since expressed. I hope that it will not be felt undignified to include this feature in England's leading newspaper.

Sir, —Let me entreat you to keep *The Times* from puzzles of all sorts. Space there is precious and prestige also.

Tuesday, January 21, 1930

Sir, —I add a plea for the inclusion of a weekly cross-word in *The Times*. These puzzles, if the numbers and clues be clearly printed, bring interest and pleasure to many invalids. To many persons these clever puzzles are an enjoyment second only to the best programmes of the BBC.

Sir, —A really clever cross-word puzzle, with well-thought-clues, is not an undignified thing, and I do not consider it would be derogatory for *The Times* to issue one. People are apt to place all cross-words in the same category and so judge hastily.

Sir, —I beg you not to allow cross-word puzzles to creep into *The Times*. I am a young woman and do not dislike all innovations; but I hate to see a great newspaper pandering to the modern craze for passing the time in all kinds of stupid ways.

Sir, —Do please keep out cross-word puzzles from your columns. There are plenty elsewhere for those of us who enjoy them. *The Times* occupies a unique position, and I am sure thousands are jealous of its being associated for one moment with guessing contests.

Wednesday, January 22, 1930

Sir, —I do hope *The Times* will give us a good research cross-word puzzle every day. The idea of its being undignified is absurd. *The Times*, I have no doubt, will add to the dignity of cross-words.

Sir, —Cross-word puzzles by all means and almost everywhere, say I, as a devotee and daily worker in that field. But not in *The Times*, surely!

THE THIRTIES

A DAILY PUZZLE IN THE TIMES, 1930

The institution of a weekly crossword puzzle in The Times *has brought a widespread demand from readers for a daily puzzle.*

A new series will therefore be begun in The Times of Saturday, *February 1, and will continue every day. The solution of each puzzle will be given in the issue following its publication.*

Spinners will make every effort to minimize the local hardship involved in their decision to close the York plant. The plant in question is the flour mill known as Leetham's Mill, York.

Justice to visit such a remote county as Cornwall. His LORDSHIP, in reply, said it was a great delight to him to come there at any time, and his only regret was that he had not been able to come earlier.

CROSSWORD PUZZLE NO. 1

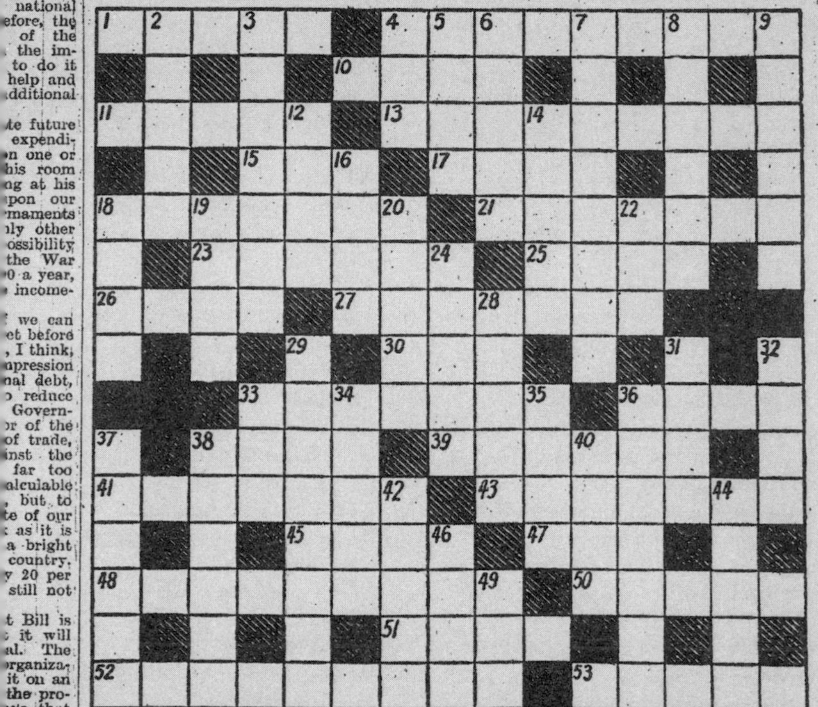

ACROSS

1 Spread unevenly.
4 Part of a Milton title.
10 A month, nothing more, in Ireland.
11 He won't settle down.
13 22 down should be this.
15 Cotton onto, so to speak.
17 Head of a chapter.
18 Denizen of the ultimate ditch.
21 Frequently under observation.
23 What's in this stands out.
25 Flighty word.
26 If the end of this gets in the way the whole may result.
27 Retunes (anag.).
30 This means study.
33 Simply enormous.
36 There's a lot in this voice.
38 This elephant has lost his head.
39 A turn for the worse.
41 Done with a coarse file.
43 Red loam (anag.).
45 This rodent's going back.
47 Makes a plaything with its past.
48 Wants confidence.
50 A mixed welcome means getting the bird.
51 This girl seems to be eating backwards.
52 The men in the moon.
53 A pinch of sand will make it dry.

DOWN

2 Heraldic gold between mother and me.
3 Out of countenance.
4 Upset this value and get a sharp reproof.
5 Intently watched.
6 In some hands the things become trumpets.
7 A religious service.
8 This horseman has dropped an h.
9 Sounds like a curious song.
12 This ought to be square.
14 Momentary stoppage.
16 Written briefly.
18 Calverley's picturesque scholars carved their names on every one.
19 Site of 45 across.
20 Precedes advantage.
22 Parents in a negative way.
24 Used to be somewhere in France.
28 Happen afterwards
29 Climbing instinct in man.
31 A terrestrial glider
32 The final crack.
33 The little devil's on our money.
34 Simplest creature.
35 Time measurements.
36 Jollier than 4 across.
37 Ladies in promising mood.
38 Presents are commonly this.
40 Gets the boot.
42 Hail in Scotland may mean tears.
44 Works, but usually plays.
46 She's dead.
49 Only a contortionist could do this on a chair.

The second crossword puzzle in this series together with the solution of puzzle No. 1, will appear in *The Times* on Monday.

Across

1. Very useful on the field, whatever Labour leaders may think (two words)
5. This is frequently quoted
9. Enter in a college (anag.) (two words)
10. If there is anything in the proverb the taxpayer should call it
11. It seems strange that every one should be trying to make him cross
13. A woman of little worth, who is now related to 5 across
15. A good 28 or a little 8, as one prefers
17. Not the sort of seat one gets in the House (two words)
19. A matter for rueful contemplation for some people to-morrow night
20. The sort of mandate asked for
21. A standard of comparison in general currency
22. The new one, of course, will make sweeping changes
23. An incomplete and distorted fact. Would Mr. Snowden give it to his colleagues who took to flight?
26. My return is one, says every candidate
27. Go out? In this case it may mean go in
28. Whatever may happen to trade, the Prime Minister wants this to be free
31. All that really matters now (four words)
32. His room is in the Lords, of course
33. Used, no doubt, with great effect by 6

Down

1. Every 11 should act according to his
2. Bankers' ramp? Result of extravagance? It's a matter of opinion (two words)
3. All parties in the election have spoken on this less
4. Naval part of a North Country constituency
5. A matter of local arrangement
6. These have all been advocating the cause of the National Government (two words)
7. There has been a big crop, chiefly about what ex-Ministers did
8. Is it a libel that MPs do sometimes during debates?
12. Not, it is urged, the main 27. In any case they have received very Churt treatment
14. Even Governments are, they say
16. Should such sorrows be lessened? That is the question
18. Perth and Belper, two dissimilar constituencies, have this in common
19. Our adhesion is needed to make this party complete
21. Clydesiders, no doubt, would agree that Parliamentary manners make a rum code
23. It is a constituency, of course, but does the football fan care?
24. Free-traders fear that this sort of duty may become a habit
25. 11 should legally be one of these
29. The little country really seems now to have its head out of action
30. In her case Jacob might have found the alternative vote useful

26 OCTOBER 1931

PRIME MINISTER'S TRIUMPH. RAMSAY MACDONALD'S NATIONAL PARTY GAINS EVERYWHERE

Across

1. He doesn't get into hot water; it's the other way about
4. The campaigner has little credit with the States and returns flushed
10. Ten? Not I (anag.)
11. House with a mason in
12. Ian in a rut (anag.)
13. I'm absent from the force, but not off the beat
14. A defence for the soldier or weapon for the miscreant
16. Send out a late drink
18. I'm on agreement in this meeting
21. He follows the field in important engagements
24. Quite possibly a Hun about fifty
25. A one-armed beast that is a quadruped
27. One may at the ironmonger's or one does in the playground
28. Wander after material for censure
29. Even the most improvident can pay these
30. Prize poles

Down

1. A robber, not reduced prize money
2. Must Continental boarders live in open sin?
3. A plant from the New World
5. Tale of a broken vessel in the City
6. It seems that the musician with grit gets the bird
7. A man with considerable powers of penetration
8. An old 1 across
9. Believing proverbially
15. The hairdresser cannot give you this, though he will get as near as possible
17. In charity reverse the scene of divorce
19. Their work is one continual grind
20. Conveyance
21. 'These to his——since he held them dear' (Tennyson)
22. Mound
23. He sounds a cheery sort of solider
26. Drank up

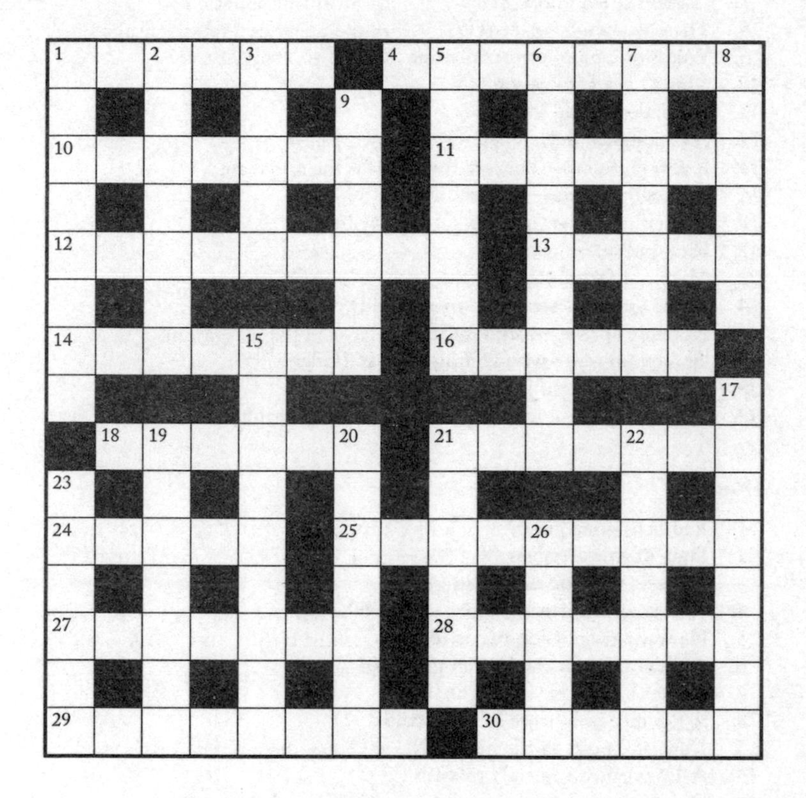

14 APRIL 1932

COCKCROFT AND WALTON SPLIT THE ATOM

Across

1. Highest speed at sea? (7)
5. These women go on foot (7)
9. Words of reproof to oarsmen for riding (two words) (6, 3)
10. This 23 is a famous song (5)
11. Grounded in bed (4)
12. A conditional detachment (10)
14. It also presumably displays the goods (8)
15. Naturally ye mist—in this dilemma (6)
18. In their trade they get a rise every day (6)
19. Rich and full in wine (8)
22. Matter of fact mood (10)
24. In the Great Western the town would counsel caution (4)
26. Example of relief-work for artists (5)
27. 'Something —— with boiling oil in it' (Gilbert) (9)
28. This female might have been *née* Sims (7)
29. Was it with these that they won the Championship? (7)

Down

1. Red hats (anag.) (7)
2. Duty of a tire repairer (9)
3. Part of a humane education (4)
4. Non-stop, but hardly express, in the fable (8)
5. He was a trifle damp inside (6)
6. Ted's in time for the French girls (10)
7. Shelter behind me in a fight (5)
8. A PC hidden in trees is insubstantial (7)
13. Defensive posts in the field (10)
16. A 17 radiance is merely rubbish (9)
17. 'One of those —— days that cannot die' (Wordsworth) (8)
18. It is often full of grub (two words) (4, 3)
20. Their work is absorbing (7)
21. Hawkers like to empty them, actors to fill them (6)
23. So the maid might urge the mistress to carry out her desire (5)
25. For his share he likes a drop (4)

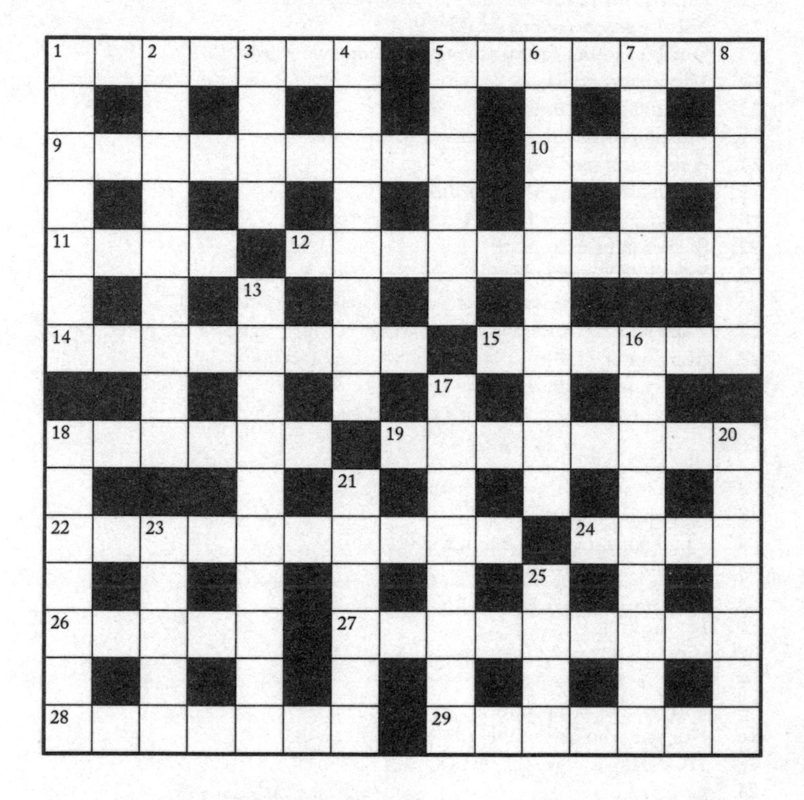

14 OCTOBER 1933

GERMANY WITHDRAWS FROM THE LEAGUE OF NATIONS

Across

1. Participator in many a dust-up (two words) (6,7)
10. No one is prepared to do this (9)
11. Suitable clothes for first thing in the morning (5)
12. 19 probably is (6)
13. He might have been caviare (8)
15. This intervened during the War (two words) (6,4)
17. A bay on a bowl (4)
19. Suitable name for the right back? (4)
20. A kingly copper is Herb (10)
22. A woman of destiny (8)
23. Bolted, followed by detectives (6)
26. This and itself alike (5)
27. There's all the difference in the world between this and the other one (two words) (5,4)
28. A loud, flashy affair (13)

Down

2. Time's up, pass the drink round (5)
3. A soup tin (anag.) (8)
4. The French have a hand in the sea (4)
5. Officer, or a departed householder? (10)
6. This butter might give a groan (6)
7. It's the limit (9)
8. Celestial utterance (two words) (6,7)
9. Señoras (two words) (7,6)
14. Anagram of Lena 12 (10)
16. Not one who gives tuition by post (9)
18. He usually follows the text (8)
21. Conduct (6)
24. Wood on credit makes a gruff sound (5)
25. Their god can be made from them (4)

6 JULY 1934

FRED PERRY WINS WIMBLEDON

Across

3. A majestic form in the courts (two words) (5,5)
8. She leaves all the show to her mate (6)
9. Cases of apprehension without reason (10)
10. This fox is a bat and was a horse (6)
11. Famous play-house (10)
12. Not, we hope, a person to neglect the issue (6)
15. Good weather to the SSE (7)
16. Implement used by a gentlemanly scribe (6)
19. Conveyance by post (6)
23. A first-rate thing to have (7)
27. Racy adjective (6)
28. Err on beach (anag.) (10)
29. Arrange again the place to go to (6)
30. Three words for two made one (3,3,4)
31. One lives on and should live within it (6)
32. Let us hope they pride themselves on their good form (10)

Down

1. One item in a cheering brew (7)
2. Absolved (7)
3. They never will go straight (7)
4. Sounds like the speed at which 3 down move (7)
5. Instead it might be instead (7)
6. Revolutionary exports of high class (7)
7. Study den (7)
13. She reminds one of Hudson (4)
14. Four points to see in the papers (4)
17. By the sound of it you're a woolworker (4)
18. Here's an Asiatic, after father (4)
20. Is this for hanging the kettle on? (7)
21. Is so upset about the legal profession (7)
22. Red loam (anag.) (7)
23. A timeserver (7)
24. A lady who has good looks? (7)
25. Order of 3 down (7)
26. 'Neither a borrower nor a lender be' does not apply here (7)

■	1	■	2	■	3		4		5		6		7	
8						■		■		■		■		■
■		■		■	9									
10						■		■		■		■		■
■		■		■	11									
12		13		14		■		■		■		■		■
■	15							■	16	17		18		
■	■		■		■	■	■	■	■		■		■	■
19	20		21		22	■	23		24		25		26	■
■		■		■		■		■	27					
28										■		■		■
■		■		■		■		■	29					
30										■		■		■
■		■		■		■		■	31					
32										■		■		■

16 MARCH 1935

HITLER INTRODUCES CONSCRIPTION

Across

1. One who tries to put the earn into learn? (two words) (5,7)
8. Tarries for musicians (5)
9. Fashionable widow's wear? (9)
11. Allow space for a non-resident (two words) (5,4)
12. A lamentable country, by the sound of it (5)
13. Molly who is certainly no tomboy (7)
15. Clues should be (7)
17. A hat in victory, a sponge in defeat (two words) (5,2)
19. Stops (7)
20. His garden book was done by Robert Hichens (5)
22. Diffused by Florence Nightingale (9)
24. It may take a lot out of one (9)
25. Sign from heaven for a Roman to depart (5)
26. These flowers, at any rate, should be proof against frost (three words) (3,3,6)

Down

1. What Philip and she do? (9)
2. Capable body (5)
3. Did they wear black togas? (7)
4. Points of difficulty in games perhaps (7)
5. Dances (unsteadily if tipsy) (two words) (4,5)
6. It sounds rather like Christmas in Surrey (5)
7. Chalet in London (two words) (5,7)
10. Edison paints (anag.) (12)
14. Not quite the ecclesiastical party one would expect to find at Upminster (two words) (3,6)
16. They should make ideal wives (two words) (4,5)
18. He can only practise with open-handed clients (7)
19. This place puts order into a yellow dog (7)
21. Good for turning but insufficient for washing (5)
23. Stage (5)

11 DECEMBER 1936

EDWARD VIII ABDICATES THE THRONE

Across

1. Eve in nautical garb (two words) (5, 4)
6. What might be an asset seems more than necessary (5)
9. Gate money derived from a change of ground? (7)
10. Submarine growth is necessarily naval expansion (7)
11. Music-hall might suggest the name (5)
12. Quick way to get big crops? (two words) (5, 4)
13. How the hospital grows, but not for in-patients (8)
14. Companion of the Bath (6)
17. What women become when they take tea (two words) (3, 3)
18. Source of Dutch courage? (8)
20. Slackness (9)
22. Seaside wear (5)
24. Street I find in Italy (7)
25. Shocking initial loss for a storyteller (7)
26. Wrong again, by gum! (5)
27. Spare seat (anag.) (9)

Down

1. Will you make a fourth at bridge? (5)
2. They don't always do good turns (15)
3. Great need for juvenile reform (two words) (6, 3)
4. The poet seems almost to have laboured under a physical disability (8)
5. You must collar us at the station (6)
6. Lead off frightened (5)
7. The crisis is so boring (three words) (3,7,5)
8. Not used by 'One who never turned his back but marched breast forward' (9)
13. Open-air life seems to benefit the tradesman (9)
15. Vehicle for a few coppers (two words) (6, 3)
16. Hull, perhaps (8)
19. More blessed folk (6)
21. Doll's-house maker (5)
23. They only show their faces after six (5)

28 MAY 1937

NEVILLE CHAMBERLAIN BECOMES PRIME MINISTER

Across

1. For comings and goings (two words) (6,7)
10. A constitutional course (four words) (3,3,4,5)
11. It forms attachments in the garden (7)
12. Press on (7)
13. I spy peel (anag.) (8)
14. Applicable to a hard saying? (6)
16. Minority (6)
18. It occupies cart room (8)
21. No; it might be a fur sale (7)
22. Bay of defeat (7)
23. The sort of vessel which is used in caravans (four words) (4,2,3,6)
24. A useful utensil, but could a bird be taught to use it? (two words) (7,6)

Down

2. Welcomed by debtors, except as a punishment (three words) (9,2,4)
3. Run even when put to confusion (7)
4. Good government means nothing to him (8)
5. Relating to a foot (6)
6. The stonebreaker seems to have a sleepy job (7)
7. Teaching teacher (two words) (8,7)
8. Down-under it's up-over (two words) (8,5)
9. Housing expenses of the bottom dog? (13)
15. Death of the penitent (two words) (5,3)
17. Travel to play in Hants (7)
19. A little work on the newspapers (7)
20. The first sunflower (6)

29 SEPTEMBER 1938

ELEVENTH-HOUR PEACE MOVE AS FOUR POWERS MEET IN MUNICH

Across

1. Whereby a murmur of revolution comes to children's ears (10)
8. It isn't penal (5)
9. Untiringly tiresome (10)
10. It is out of joint (5)
11. Part of Scotland is kin to it (4)
12. It's pretty but often rough at the edges (7)
15. Name I met (anag.) (8)
16. Cartoonist, formerly doctor (5)
19. It isn't cricket, or is it? (5)
20. Mountain of Light (8)
23. Take up husbandry perhaps (7)
24. Refreshments for sale (4)
25. Industrial or horticultural (5)
27. Scene of 'Shall We Join the Ladies?' (10)
28. Sandy seems to hurry away empty (5)
29. Game that winners of the Dunmow Flitch might indulge in (10)

Down

1. When he gets round Alf and Tim (8)
2. Ecclesiastic refused Minorca by the French (two words) (5, 5)
3. Where the American does not disclose the extent of his indebtedness (4)
4. Bobby abroad (8)
5. Porter's nom de plume (two words) (1, 5)
6. Standard of tan (5)
7. Forgo with a gesture (5)
10. French general (7)
13. He might express gracefully the unlevelness of a hovel (7)
14. Where one would be surrounded by people of one's own class (10)
17. Not young Tommy's idea of 'control' (8)
18. The fellow has an urge to his vocation (8)
21. One who gave up a habit for the good of others (6)
22. Composer with a certain amount of good luck (5)
23. Enter the lists, as it were (5)
26. The Taj Mahal is there (4)

1 SEPTEMBER 1939

NAZI GERMANY INVADES POLAND

SPECULATION ABOUT THE FIRST COMPILERS

There has always been conjecture about the identity of crossword compilers. Much curiosity was aroused about the first compiler and letters were regularly received at The Times *guessing at his character.*

Who is he? According to the correspondence which comes into Printing House Square, he is a clergyman (possibly a canon), educated at Eton and Oxford, and a member of the Pickwick Club; he enjoys private theatricals, does not like gardening, and is a Boer War veteran. It appears that somewhere in this curriculum vitae, he has found some time for some education at Winchester, to be admitted to the Bar, and become a member of the Royal Horticultural Society. He is reputed to live in London or the country; if the latter, then he has no knowledge of it.

WHO COMPILED THIS ONE, THEN?

Times Crosswords never acknowledge their authorship, not even by way of the pseudonyms used in other papers. Why is this? In the early days, it was merely following the general custom in the paper that nothing was attributed to an individual writer. Indeed, our first compiler, Adrian Bell, was expected to keep his authorship secret even from his own acquaintances. Nowadays, the names of our team are no secret – a group photograph captioned with all our names appeared in the paper in the spring of 2005. But we still do not identify the author of each day's puzzle. Partly this is the inertia of tradition; but there are some advantages. Some solvers may find over time that they prefer some compilers to others, so that they may not bother at all with the puzzle on some days, or on others start with a sinking feeling of inadequacy that makes what they expect to be a difficult puzzle even more so. With no such hints, solvers are encouraged to attempt every day's puzzle, and to do so without preconceptions. (Except perhaps the widely held idea, true once perhaps but no longer, that the puzzle is of graded difficulty through the week, starting with an easy Monday and finishing with a fiendish Saturday.)

A second point is that it is easier to edit an unnamed puzzle, because the compiler does not have to feel that something that is 'not his' is put out under his name, and thus a much more consistent style and standard can be achieved in what is always '*The Times* Crossword', not an individual's crossword that happens to appear in *The Times*. Indeed, even seasoned solvers can be wildly wrong in attempting to pin authorship of any particular puzzle on to someone whose hand they think they recognize. Our team regularly debates whether we should join the majority and put a name to each puzzle; but so far we have always decided that the advantages of anonymity outweigh the disadvantages, so the puzzle remains for at least the foreseeable future, as it has been throughout its first seventy-five years, just *The Times* Crossword.

Richard Browne

ADRIAN BELL

The First Compiler of The Times Crossword
1930–1980

Birth of The Times Crossword Puzzle

I was commissioned to produce within a month six crossword puzzles of a type that should not affront the dignity of *The Times* readership, or belittle the presumably well-stocked mind of the literary heritage of our ruling class.

But to unload daily a crossword puzzle upon, say, the Athenaeum Club, the Reform Club, the Carlton Club and all the august establishments of St James's, was too big a dare. My six puzzles were composed simply for *The Times* Weekly Edition, which went to all the outposts of Empire around the globe. Thus, the reverberation of 'What! A crossword puzzle in *The Times*?' would filter slowly back home in muted shock waves – a sort of underground test, so to speak.

Adrian Bell, 1980

Bell was a prolific writer of books on English rural life and of character, gentle, modest and wise. One can see a nice capacity for lateral thinking in one of his books where he asks his wife, who is hanging over the marmalade pan, 'What happened to the wooden spoon the cat gave you for Christmas?'. Crossword compiling, he said, was 'the ideal job for a chap with a vacant mind sitting on a tractor harrowing clods or bicycling'. Most of his work seems to have been done on his bicycle in country lanes, with the chosen words for his next crossword propped up in the basket in front of him.

In his early puzzles he was plainly more concerned with familiarizing readers with the crossword idea than in being cryptic. But his ability to look at things in a new light soon became apparent: '*The cylinder is jammed (5, 4)*' for example [SWISS ROLL]. And has anyone ever produced two neater clues than '*Die of cold (3, 4)*' and '*Spoils of War (4)*' [ICE CUBE and MARS]?

John Grant, 1990

All that I can add is the memory of mother standing at the gas stove in Beccles, spoon in one hand stirring a saucepan and pencil in the other hand doing a crossword scheme; and Colin on his first visit to Beccles expressing an admiring interest in father's authorship of crosswords, to which father replied, 'A complete waste of time, dear boy'.

Sylvia Proudman, 2005, daughter of Adrian Bell, recounting the first time she introduced her future husband, Colin, to her father.

RONALD CARTON
First Editor of The Times Crossword
1930–1960

Reminiscences of Polly Tatum, Daughter of Ronald Carton

'Ubiquitous. What can I say about ubiquitous?' my father sighed.

'All over the place,' I suggested.

'That will do nicely,' he said and wrote my clue into his crossword puzzle. I was eleven and proud. My younger brother Geoffrey and I were gradually drawn into the world of clues and puns and alternative spellings, dictionaries, gazetteers, and quotations. My father's involvement with 'cwps' began in 1930 and lasted until his death thirty years later. My mother had always helped him and when he died she continued where he had left off. Literally, for she moved to his desk. Father always advised us not to get involved, but my brother did not heed the advice and, to this day, he supplies a puzzle to another journal.

As often as not our parents and their books were not in the same place, indeed they were often on different floors of the house. We didn't always enjoy helping but it was good training in the use of reference books and they say that running up and down stairs keeps you fit. I have never weighed Webster's dictionary but I can assure you it is very heavy.

During the war the crosswords were composed in extraordinary and even funny circumstances. Father was a wit but as every stand-up comedian knows it isn't easy to be funny all the time. Whenever a bomb fell in our part of London mother had to get to the scene as fast as she could to take up point duty with the WVS. Sometimes she would be gone for several days at a time. So while she stood in smoking rubble in the Holloway Road organizing, informing and comforting, father stood at the kitchen stove making our supper and composing clever crosswords with funny clues. How did he do it? Well, he had a reading audience of thousands and as an entertainer he couldn't let them down. I think it was more the spirit of show-business that kept him going. More solemn people may call it duty. Call it what you will, it is the same spirit that enables an unhappy comedian to make you laugh, a tired athlete to finish the race, and even an editor to produce 600 words by morning when he's abed with the 'flu'. Every night at 5.25 father would telephone Printing House Square with the corrections for tomorrow's puzzle. I think he was only late once – he had difficulty making a telephone connection from Switzerland. His sense of duty was so strong that when he died we found that he had left a fortnight's supply of puzzles in his desk all ready for the printer.

THE TIMES OBITUARY: MR RONALD CARTON
July 11th 1960

... The puzzles were produced in circumstances during the war that were sometimes ludicrous and sometimes near tragic. Carton himself, as well as editing the feature (no puzzle ever appeared that had not been subject to his scrutiny), contributed the bulk of the puzzles to *The Times*, and the credit for their large following, and the manifest pleasure they provide has been entirely his. His correspondence was large and varied and came from all over the world. It was not unusual to receive a letter complaining of the obscurity of a clue, to be followed a few hours later by a telegram from the repentant solver indicating that he had just seen the point and was laughing his head off.

But I shall always feel that his greatest achievement was the establishment of the Crossword Puzzle – much to the horror of some of the old gentlemen in the Pall Mall clubs who told the Editor very forcibly that *The Times* was going to the dogs. There was, for a time, some doubt as to whether the feature would be continued but it was providential that at that moment *The Times* tripped up with a clue that muddled up Casca with Cassius. The storm of shocked protests which reached the office persuaded the Editor that the Crossword Puzzle must go on.

During the Second World War, Carton worked in a government department on anti-enemy propaganda, but somehow managed to contribute the bulk of the crosswords as well as edit them all. When the office started making cuts in the clues, on the grounds of the paper shortage, he was moved to protest that '... the clues of the crossword are written, and always have been written, with the greatest economy of words. That is what makes them bright and pungent. To cut down what is already succinct is to impair the general quality of the work.'

John Grant, 1990

THE FORTIES

Across

1. What to do between I and K (8)
5. Wine at the health resort (6)
9. 'Trip no further pretty —— Journeys end in lovers meeting' (Shakespeare) (8)
10. Two policemen make this coin (6)
12. It makes very little difference to a he cub (6)
13. This puts the lid on many a fruity product (8)
15. By way of an exciting experience, perhaps (12)
18. A Dickensian was particularly impressed, apparently, by its milestones (three words) (3, 5, 4)
23. Meredith's was an amazing one (8)
24. A trophy for the champion layer? (6)
26. A starting point (6)
27. Things can be arranged so that one's born in a university (8)
28. A sort of medical invitation to the vocalist (6)
29. The medical officer joins the ladies,—how perfectly sweet! (8)

Down

1. A chap's an officer in Turkey (6)
2. Interlace (6)
3. Distinguished but incompetent (7)
4. A short extract from Matthew Arnold (4)
6. Famous bird of passage navigated by another famous bird (7)
7. 'Dost thou think, because thou art ——, there shall be no more cakes and ale?' (Shakespeare) (8)
8. It is followed this year by a number of thieves (8)
11. Does this describe Argentina? (7)
14. 4 gem (anag.) (7)
16. Harold won it with bridge and Edward IV without (8)
17. Near firs (anag.) (8)
19. An address to the wing is what one has in mind (7)
20. 'For he by geometric scale could take the size of pots of ale, and wisely tell what hour o' th' day the clock does strike by ——' (Butler) (7)
21. Men are employed to shift them (6)
22. Hastens (6)
25. Given in response to 28 (4)

1 2 3 4 5 6 7 8
9 10
11
12 13
14
15
16 17
18 19 20
21 22
23 24
25
26 27
28 29

21 AUGUST 1940

TROTSKY ASSASSINATED IN MEXICO CITY

Across

1. Calvin gets a blow instead of wine (8)
5. Estimate for Jenny (6)
10. Mrs Proudie's slippery henchman (5)
11. Catch sight of an expert? (9)
12. Enduring (7)
14. 'O, it came o'er my ear like the sweet south,
That breathes upon a bank of ——' (Shakespeare: *Twelfth Night*) (7)
15. Lion's anger (anag.) (10)
16. Manx stoat in the hall (4)
19. What to do to the frumious bandersnatch (4)
21. One might almost think they take it lying down (10)
24. 'Nelson's peerless name' (7)
25. 'She is a woman, therefore, may be won; She is ——,
therefore must be loved' (Shakespeare: *T. Andron.*) (7)
26. These hawkers don't push barrows (9)
28. A Field-Marshal doesn't eat his (5)
29. Leap Year fiancés? (6)
30. Pier romp shouldn't be like this (8)

Down

1. No doubt these people would be glad if somebody just
dropped them a line (9)
2. The glass of fashion and fantasy (7)
3. 'Drones suck not eagles' blood, but rob ——'
(Shakespeare: *2 Henry VI*) (8)
4. It doesn't undermine the tree (3)
6. A drunkard takes a glutton to heart (6)
7. A little officer caught in the way out (7)
8. They sink in time (5)
9. A cloven nut (anag.) (10)
13. Branch establishments in the illumination business (10)
17. Though he pledges himself, he seems unable to pledge others (9)
18. This part of Southampton suggests the Bench (two words) (5, 3)
20. Lino does (7)
22. *Perpetuum mobile* (7)
23. 'Henry the Eighth, life, honour, name, and all That made me happy, at one
—— has taken For ever from the world' (Shakespeare: *Henry VIII*) (6)
24. Querulous at draughts? (5)
27. Who dared to call Dr Johnson this? (3)

11 DECEMBER 1941

US DECLARES WAR ON GERMANY

Across

1. Somewhat vulgar young females, of respectable character (10)
6. Bed-book (4)
10. One of Elgar's arrangements (5)
11. 'The fatal bellman, which gives the stern'st goodnight' (Shakespeare: *Macbeth*) (3)
12. 7, perhaps (5)
13. Voluntary exile (6)
14. Even if he were freed from his pains, he would still be ill (8)
16. Crooks in the ghetto? (9)
17. Philadelphia would have been no place for him (4)
20. Even one of the fair sex may be (4)
22. Senior and junior counsel, perhaps, in collaboration? (9)
26. The 'Mammoth Trees' of California (8)
27. Eat it and you will find it anything but (6)
29. 'The feathers nodded in the breeze, And made a gallant ——' (Wordsworth) (5)

32, 30. It's always flag day, so far as this is concerned (7)

31. More than a specimen of Melville's writing (5)
33. If given a wide berth, one might be glad of this too (10)

Down

1. Driving should be one of his accomplishments (6)
2. Fuel mostly what it will do (7)
3. Battle array? (8)
4. Bird in the corner (4)
5. Hotel price (anag.) (10)
7. 10 travels up with a first-class return (7)
8. Begum, a river (8)
9. Security in tangible form (5)
15. Crazy with an automobile driven apparently on American petrol (10)
18. 11's fellow-voyager (8)
19. They provide a Scot with a winding-sheet (8)
21. A mystery writer (two words) (2, 5)
23. One might fancy a dark horse for these stakes (7)
24. If you hold this you can't keep (5)
25. this (6)
28. A title of respect, however you look at it (4)

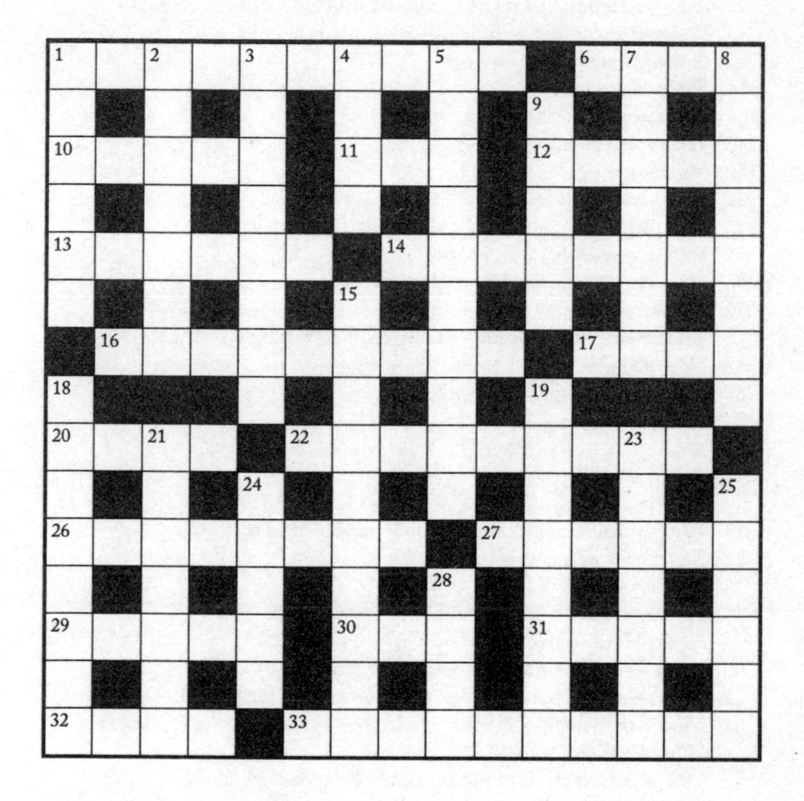

1 JANUARY 1942

DECLARATION OF U.N. SIGNED BY 26 COUNTRIES

Across

2. Assyrian reconstruction of Chinese barn (11)
9. It would make things difficult for the medical profession (7)
10. A winner at Cruft's? (3, 4)
11. Slight change (6)
12. Enigma as medicine (8)
14. The record of a downfall (9)
15. See 26
19. Try a hard case (4)
20. How the team spirit may be displayed, incidentally, on the football field (2, 7)
23. Supervisor of an underground system (8)
25. A word of entreaty (6)
27. 'A little —— flower, Before milk-white, now purple with Love's wound' (*M.N.D.*) (7)
28. A Scot and so on (7)
29. Peter's choir (anag.) (11)

Down

1. William Rufus could not truthfully have said so (6)
2. Punctuality was engrained in it (9)
3. My lady in a book (8)
4. He might have helped, possibly, to stem the flood (4)
5. Agnes Hardy (anag.) (10)
6. From whom one might expect to get a ruling (6)
7. Miss —— was not Charley's aunt, fortunately for her (5)
8. 'Most rich, being poor; Most choice —— ; and most loved, despised' (*King Lear*) (8)
13. One is not expected to put on court dress for it (4, 6)
16. Here there would be enough and to spare if the embargo were lifted (9)
17. Elusive journeyman (8)
18. Browning's last poems (8)
21. 'Now slides the silent —— on, and leaves A shining furrow' (Tennyson) (6)
22. It never lacks support (6)
24. Trees may be as razors (5)

26, 15. Matey (8)

2 FEBRUARY 1943

GERMANS SURRENDER AT STALINGRAD

Across

1. Best disturbed by conceit (8)
5. A difficult ascent, when very short (4, 2)
10. A tricky cornet cue for a player (6, 9)
11. Unpinned (7)
12. Proverbially hard workers (7)
13. A loud opponent of the 12 (7)
14. Our own has an annual circulation (6)
17. How the rent may be got together (6)
19. It is useless for collecting purposes (3, 4)
23. Why! It is something to remember in slang (4, 3)
24. He is put down by another (7)
25. Military equivalent, perhaps, of a sea lawyer (8, 7)
26. Seamless needleworker (6)
27. Keeps on (8)

Down

1. The harvest moon? (6)
2. The medicine to obtain is material (7)
3. Position of the man who is again losing his job (7, 3, 5)
4. The friar's dance (8)
6. Gold went? Sack men (anag.) (15)
7. What the athlete does when the test is over? (7)
8. Where rubber is grown? (8)
9. County collapses (5)
15. Where Jim, the fireguard, drinks (8)
16. His trust is in Scotland (8)
18. Men run when he shoots (7)
20. Ran up in a swarm (7)
21. Quick work for the lawyer (5)
22. A shell exploded, and where (6)

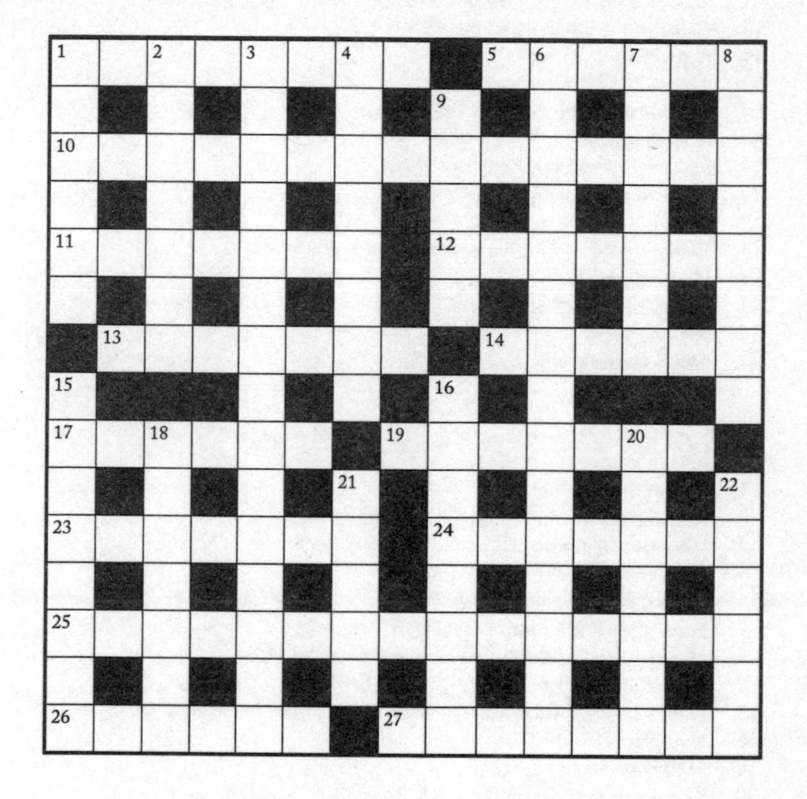

27 JANUARY 1944

LENINGRAD SIEGE ENDS AFTER 900 DAYS

Across

1. Sounds a shady way for the musician to avoid getting flat (5,8)
10. Cause of the whale's blubber? (7)
11. A coach in Scotland (7)
12. Tom is not a dry customer (5)
13. The highest post to which the sailor may aspire (9)
14. A swell gem (9)
16. Part of the Amazon Estuary (5)
17. Scene of the underground movement (5)
19. Is their waking a matter of clockwork? (9)
21. Evidently Waller did his beloved to a rose (9)
24. Under water (5)
25. What they do in Arundel? (7)
26. African river (7)
27. Not necessarily won by craft (13)

Down

2. A worrying dog (7)
3. It is responsible for a hold-up in housing (4, 5)
4. 19's stock-in-trade? (5)
5. Dora and me (anag.) (9)
6. Hard if novel (5)
7. Poetical even after humbug (7)
8. He sang 'Beautiful soup, so rich and green' (3, 4, 6)
9. Article of drawing-room furniture? (8, 5)
15. King Charles doesn't seem to have lost his head in Belgium (9)
16. Kim played on it (3,6)
18. Medicinal metal (7)
20. The opposite of a rough bed (5, 2)
22. A reverse doesn't change her (5)
23. Unlucky for the baker? (5)

1 2 3 4 5 6 7 8 9 10 11 12 13 14 15 16 17 18 19 20 21 22 23 24 25 26 27

1 MAY 1945

HITLER DEAD: FÜHRER 'HAS FALLEN AT HIS COMMAND POST'

Across

1. Arrive too late, —for the girl conductor (4, 3, 3)
9. A theme of Sheridan's (7)
10. Where the ogre's vines make money (10)
11. This book is the Book of Acts (7)
12. Not a member of the CID (8)
13. Citadel of the Eastern front (7)
14. Mates in a ship (10)
20. One way to get him is to burn the heather (10)
21. They come in a light shower (7)
22. One would expect this story by Chesterton to be full of expression (8)
23. Apollo beat him and skinned him (7)
25. Absolved with water (10)
26. Not a gem (anag.) (7)
27. Money down? (10)

Down

1. Spoil and adorn in a ship (8)
2. Make a temporary economy (4, 4)
3. He suggests the reverse of a good habit (8)
4. Sailor diet (anag.) (10)
5. Vessels for the Navy in the States (4)
6. Judy O'Grady and the Colonel's lady (7)
7. Some six years recently, though once it was a hundred (7)
8. It's not lacking in brain (7)
13. Such turns are striking displays (10)
15. Get me a table for him (8)
16. Crime that cancels 22 (8)
17. That gained by an unopposed return? (4, 4)
18. Receptacle in wood on one side of the choir (7)
19. Spicy times (7)
20. Cleaned in confession (7)
24. This black is a man of polish (4)

5 MARCH 1946

CHURCHILL DECLARES AN 'IRON CURTAIN' HAS FALLEN 'FROM STETTIN IN THE BALTIC TO TRIESTE IN THE ADRIATIC'

Across

1. Cut down the team (8)
5. It makes a trail (6)
10. One keen on twos rather than threes (7, 8)
11. 15 when it hasn't got in (4)
12. One wouldn't long survive like this (10)
14. 'All quiet along the ——' (7)
15. Unexpected returns are announced by this bell (6)
18. That of Damocles was this sort of sword (6)
19. They might have some difficulty in toeing the line (7)
22. Tails never turn into this (5, 5)
23. Arnold wrote of its light (4)
25. Cocoa curbs a mule (anag.) (4, 2, 1, 8)
26. Shut up! What language! (6)
27. 151,000 edge tools (8)

Down

1. Coiled tractably (6)
2. Friendly race meeting (6, 2, 7)
3. Found in 22 23 (4)
4. An enlightening fracture (8)
6. They sound like arsenals (10)
7. People swear here (2, 3, 7, 3)
8. His work requires some beating (8)
9. French town for hangings (5)
13. Alongships (4, 3, 3)
16. No alternative to a steel helmet in action (8)
17. Lock by cheek (8)
20. Unfrocking sentence (5)
21. Ill-mannered engineers in the Army (6)
24. Scene of hard fighting in the Marianas (4)

15 AUGUST 1947

INDIA'S FIRST DAY OF INDEPENDENCE

Across

1. Anti-prohibitionists carry everything in cases (7)
4. Kind (7)
8. The occupation of Mr Omer of Yarmouth (11)
11. The stoic is browned off, as it were (4)
12. It's threatening if agitated (4)
13. The screen's their medium (7)
15. They seldom change (6)
16. Hope is inherent in her (6)
17. The result, if you do, might be a tonic (11)
20. He wouldn't feel at home if canonized (6)
22. It can hardly be described as an 'out-of-the-way' situation (6)
23. It's a lot, but most of it is small (7)
24. Our appearance with this two-valver would cause an outcry (4)
26. I go after it in Australia (4)
27. He should be a good judge of a lawn (11)
28. Burns (7)
29. Of course, his wealth is in his tail (7)

Down

1. Attractive, and apparently successful (7)
2. He's in a peculiar position (4)
3. Where they didn't quite make the best of it (6)
5. Problems for 15 (6)
6. No doubt he expects to rule the roast (4)
7. Definite article in seed (7)
8. Wessex year-book? (5, 6)
9. Shows what an odd case it is (11)
10. Telephonic will-o'-the-wisp (5, 6)
13. But, nevertheless, still susceptible to the cold (7)
14. Icy toes (anag.) (7)
18. Yuletide biscuit (7)
19. Grilled tomatoes, for example, in Lancashire (7)
21. Something to show concerning meat of a sort (6)
22. Low fellows (6)
25. Carriage (4)
26. Not a beast of burden (4)

14 MAY 1948

END OF PALESTINE MANDATE: NEW STATE OF ISRAEL PROCLAIMED

Across

1, 10. Sweet rationing put many of them temporarily out of action (9, 8)
11. Vessels of standard tonnage, no doubt (9)
12. Look, a ham in a certain state (8)
13. Quite a reliable cape (9)
14. Foot yarn (6)
15. Half a sheep is like a queen (9)
22. Does he belong to the country's centre party? (9)
23. A restriction that may hamper the will (6)
24. Time in which a mason dies (9)
25. It's no light thing to censor (5, 3)
26. Insects to cause a conflagration in the theatre (9)
27. Study here gets hackneyed; sorry (8)
28. One of the 9 has value in a London suburb (9)

Down

2. UNO's dole is free (8)
3. Stuffy appeal for the end of cinema music (8)
4. Attic (8)
5. These are simply not done; they can't be (15)
6. Pipes, perhaps (5)
7. While he works others, maybe, are wool-gathering (7)
8. This may keep one out of pocket (7)
9. Man's one of them (7)
16. An optical delusion (5, 3)
17. It's not an outstanding design (8)
18. Allowance in a tear (8)
19. Upstage in the film studio in reverse (7)
20. Better musical than muscular (7)
21. Andrew Jackson was old this (7)
24. Not a uniform religious leader (5)

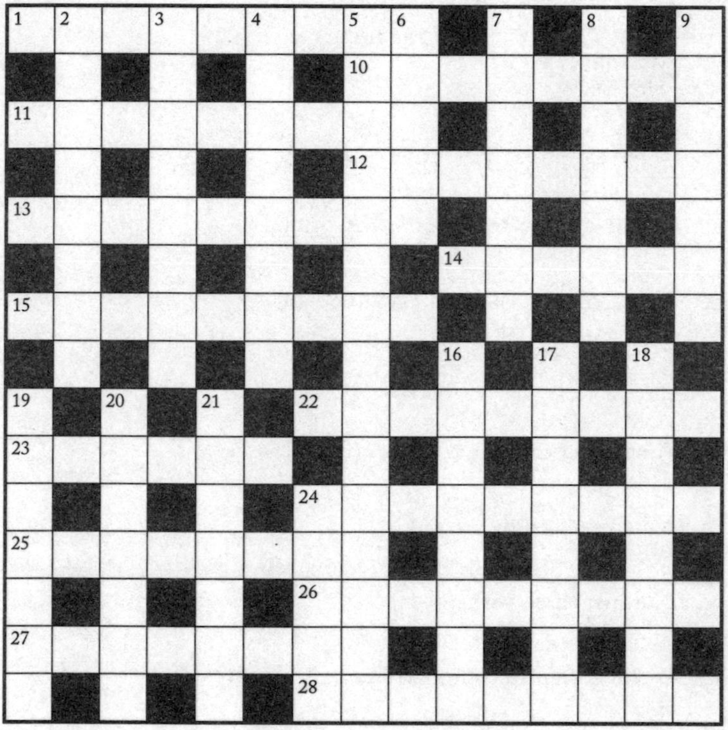

4 APRIL 1949

NORTH ATLANTIC TREATY SIGNED BY 12 NATIONS

TIMES READERS' FAVOURITE CLUES
from the last 75 years

1. What cooks do with books (5)

2. Perching birds don't when they do (4, 3)

3. He represents one, and I another (8)

4. Amundsen's forwarding address (4)

5. A rose-red city – it bombed (9)

6. Much-blessed dwarf (6)

7. Number three perhaps (5)

8. Is she got up to confound head and heart? (5)

9. Cold display unit for seafood (11)

10. Faith and character of Britten shown by his mass (8)

11. Old historian understood modern power (7)

12. Sex – it is awful? Get a life! (5)

13. Swan upping (10)

14. O for a deputy! (6,2,7)

15. Terrible summer noted by Puccini (3,4,3)

16. She takes a lot of trouble to compose her features (5, 4)

17. Safe to sleep around? A boy always results (5, 3)

18. Power to capture both rooks, giving brilliant mate (2,5)

19. When depressed, one gives no impression of character (5, 3)

20. Pot of ale (4, 5)

21. Glance at the fixtures: not much on (8)

22. Wear a rather revealing top emerging from the waves (6)

23. Very fine clues sold for a pound (9)

24. Blow me down! (9, 5)

25. Fit in girl's pockets (15)

26. Peter Pan (3, 4)

27. Performances that appealed to the gods but emptied the stalls (9)

For solutions see page 271 and 272

POEMS
about The Times Crossword

The most damning thing one can say about a crossword clue is that it could only be a crossword clue, because it reads so oddly. The art of the compiler is to make clues read logically, smoothly and innocently. Perhaps we succeed in *The Times*, for one of our solvers has been so struck by what she is pleased to call their lyrical language that she now turns them into verse. An example culled from the puzzle of April 1, 1989:

The war god has not backed Othello in battle
Tamed, perhaps and defeated
Die, we hear, as a result of scorched earth –
Funeral carriage about to arrive at the gate
(Specious order to sup with Belial).

Elena A. Dingle

From time to time she sends me new examples hot from the grid, begging me not to bother acknowledging 'because you must be busy turning carthorses into orchestras'.

John Grant, 1981

Precocious solvers, please take note,
You're really beginning to get my goat.

I'll emulate Ximenes and Torquemada,
And make the damn things very much harder.

An old hand like me knows all the tricks,
My avian's archaeopteryx.

I'm trawling all the e-mail spam,
To construct a fiendish anagram.

The vocab's got very much too simple;
All the buffs are on to 'wimple'.

But all their wiles aren't a shred of use.
You can't use words that are so abstruse.

The man on the Clapham omnibus,
Would surely kick up quite a fuss.

John Blackburn

The Crossword Cure

O nameless coiner of the cryptic clue,
O master of delusive definition
Embracing in your panoramic view
A world of miscellaneous erudition,
Once more I pay the homage due
To your wise conduct of your Inquisition,
Bringing a daily boon and breathing space
To the tired runners in a mad world's race.

You leave no fruitful avenues unexplored
That minister to innocent hilarity,
But never strike a harsh or jarring chord,
Or find a virtue in unveiled vulgarity.
Rumour and gossip are by you ignored;
You season ridicule with kindly charity,
Yet on occasion with unerring eyes
Transfix malicious folly as it flies.

You jog my memory with your mental jerks;
To you, in fine, I owe a double debt
For while the old machinery still works
And shows no sign of breaking down as yet –
Thanks to the stimulus of your quips and quirks –
You teach me to remember, and forget.
For Hell's most grisly gangsters have no power
To crash the gate that guards the Crossword hour.

B. L. Grave

This poem appeared in *The Times* on July 23, 1941, addressed to the Editor of *The Times* Crossword

Got up
Had shave
Did Times crossword

Had another shave

Roger McGough

A NEW KIND OF CROSSWORD: NIGHT THOUGHTS

The crossword puzzle printed on the next page is unusual. It is explained in the following extract from a private letter. In 1940, Sir Max Beerbohm wrote to *The Times*: 'No doubt you, like most people, have sometimes thought of some utterly awful thing that you could do if you chose to, some disastrous and devastating thing the very thought of which has brought cold sweat to your brow? And you may have at some time thought:

'"Suppose I released into the columns of *The Times*, one of these fine days, a crossword puzzle with clues signifying nothing whatsoever," and may have hideously pictured to yourself the effect on all educated parts of Great Britain?

'You may incidentally have seen yourself going into your club shortly before luncheon time and observing in the armchairs men with blank, set, fixed, pale, just-not-despairing faces, poring over the current issue? – one of them perhaps rising unsteadily and lumbering out of the library and asking the librarian, "Have we a Wordsworth concordance?", or some question of that sort...

'And you may further have wondered just how the apology in the next day's issue should be worded – just what excuse should be offered, before the shutters in Printing House Square were briskly and slammingly put up for ever? Perhaps I oughtn't to remind you of this nightmare of yours. Forgive me.

'PS: The nightmare wouldn't be loathsomely complete unless a few of the clues were genuine – and very simple, so as to put the solvers in good heart, and make them confident of success, and keep their shoulders to the wheel. I have provided six such clues, with my usual forethought.'

THE TIMES CROSSWORD PUZZLE No. ?

ACROSS

1 A Victorian statesman lurking in a side lair (8).

5 Milky way unseen by star-gazers (6).

9 An insect with a girl on each side (8).

10 Pugilists' wear (6).

11 Four toes are broken (8).

12 The cockney's goddess appears to have been a slimmer (6).

14 There's a little company in the meadow next month (10).

18 " But what if memory Itself our — — —s had betrayed ? " (Matthew Arnold) (two words) (5, 5).

22 A nudist's aunt? (6).

23 " That day he —— the Nervii " (Shakespeare) (8).

24 Acknowledgement of debt in a vessel (6).

25 Neither animal nor mineral, and only three-fourths vegetable (8).

26 Not what the wicket-keeper tries for in Essex (6).

27 The P.R.A. is utterly confounded (8).

DOWN

1 Drum (Newbolt) (6).

2 The top of the morning, perhaps (6).

3 A Manx beverage (6).

4 Ho! Let's go in (anag.) (10).

6 Wordsworth's fan mail? (8).

7 And yet sugar *can* be refined (8).

8 They are up and doing, no doubt, in "the sweet o' the year" (8).

13 Little Tommy thought it meant a red-faced blacksmith (10)

15 Voltaire's *pretre enragé* (8).

16 Such buns are eaten on a good day (two words) (3, 5).

17 Caliban's sea-change (8).

19 Pollarded haven (6).

20 I'm in the old Roman bath (6).

21 " Our —— clues that do but darken counsel " (Tennyson) (6).

Out of consideration for our solvers, *The Times* printed Beerbohm's letter alongside his crossword. Some of his clues read more like crossword clues than the real thing, and his quotations would not have disgraced their putative authors. Given this protective coloration, his six clues are not all that easy to spot.

For solutions see page 271.

LETTERS

Sir,—On a recent visit to Egypt a friend purchased a copy of *The Times* for £E 2.50 (approximately £1.25) and was delighted to find that the crossword had been accurately completed.

I have tried asking my supplier what he will charge for this remarkable service, and other readers might also be interested if you could provide details of how it can be arranged.

Mr John Ruffle, 1987

This tongue-in-cheek suggestion became reality some years later with the offer of a premium-rate phone line to provide exactly this service in 1987.

Sir, —I vividly remember, when I was a child, my father revealing on his return from his daily commute to London on the train: 'Ah, it was a tough one today, took me between Barming and Swanley to complete.'

Fran Williams, 2003

Sir, —If your correspondent leaves his copy of *The Times* on the train for others to read then that is an act of charity. If he leaves some other newspaper he is a litter lout.

If, however, he leaves his copy of *The Times* with the crossword completed then he may be suspected of being a show-off.

Mr J Bunting, 1988

THE FIFTIES

Across

1. The voice suggests the teeth are not the singer's own (8)
5. Cheeps are, of young birds (6)
10. It is the turn of the snob and the swell to appear tasteful (7)
11. The exploiter of labour seems unlikely to be cold-shouldered (7)
12. Business wrecked by anger (9)
13. Roxburgh birthplace of Thomson of 'The Seasons' (5)
14. Arnold, the writer (7)
16. He can swallow very little (7)
17. Back seats that get a theatrical light? (4,3)
20. Don't look for this in 'The Dun Cow' (4,3)
22. He is likely to receive conflicting counsel (5)
23. Among those who go in off the deep end? (2,3,4)
25. They do not as a rule announce their arrival vocally (7)
26. Hit ribs (anag.) (7)
28. Bride—groom, which? (6)
29. Not the days referred to by Hamlet in saying, 'The time is out of joint' (8)

Down

1. A terminological inexactitude (3)
2. Not Abraham's home town (7)
3. Call up a representative woman who has assimilated the correct slang (5)
4. Does it show how Parliament interfered in cricket? (4,3)
6. A single course, perhaps (9)
7. The only epithet to apply to some old fossils (7)
8. Scatter-brained state of timid, hen-pecked sheikhs? (11)
9. Easter's later beauties? (6)
12. Give Highlanders champagne and they may not survive Christmas (11)
15. Former railway employees now earning dollars in business (9)
18. Painter of our mill (7)
19. Many a country fellow has been well-rid of this (6)
20. A tumble for a change that is changeable (7)
21. East London railway that has its twists and turns (7)
24. One way in which a foreigner might think to achieve output (5)
27. Hurry up, it's ten short (3)

1 2 3 4 5 6 7 8 9 10 11 12 13 14 15 16 17 18 19 20 21 22 23 24 25 26 27 28 29

21 JANUARY 1950

GEORGE ORWELL DIES

Across

1. His contract is doubled, as it were (8)
5. Blows that yield net returns (6)
9. A politician's turning after nonsense (8)
10. My kingdom for a horse? No, only a bit of one (6)
12. A boy's the big noise in pantomime (7)
13. The lion's is like a coal, the poet said (7)
14. A chirpy marriage, no doubt (7, 5)
17. It ends in September, and the moon is dying (5, 7)
22. All those exhortations to miners? (4, 3)
23. This craft's job is to do this (7)
24. Figures, Mrs General said, of importance to speech (6)
25. Humiliating lineage (4, 4)
26. Red painter (6)
27. Change to a dress as arranged (8)

Down

1. Extremist feminine attitude of an employee (6)
2. Village that has done well with the bacon ration (6)
3. He might turn to drama in the ring (7)
4. A sinewy dish, for builders (6, 6)
6. Name wrongly and lose some schooling (7)
7. Ross's associate (8)
8. Furtive (8)
11. Junketings in rebel coats (12)
15. That habitual snooker shot (8)
16. He may have delivered a series of knockouts (8)
18. A long-lost letter to 19, perhaps (7)
19. Domenico Theotocopuli (2, 5)
20. Roman subdivision (6)
21. Fruit may be so punished (6)

26 OCTOBER 1951

WINSTON CHURCHILL VOTED IN AS PRIME MINISTER

Across

1. Cop a copper (10)
6. Man a-sitting on a gate was twice so (4)
10. Marksman's shot at dinner (5)
11. Chant by Grieg, Nora (9)
12. Tinners continue! (5)
13. Knockabout relative's friend (4,5)
14. It's State policy that all are (7)
16. They can deal with brute force (6)
19. City of cheap beef (6)
21. Here horseflesh is abounding (7)
22. A blaze of colour in the garden (9)
24. Famous as a libretto comes to be (5)
25. Curt Freda (anag.) (9)
26. May not *tutoyer* in this tongue? (5)
27. Ribbon development in fenestration (4)
28. They do not compete for the Blue Riband of the Atlantic (5,5)

Down

1. Good health or obesity (4,4)
2. Tanner with a note perhaps (3,3,3)
3. Bird much loved by Leander (5)
4. New over there (7)
5. Don't be a pauper—haven't got to (4,3)
7. Fire bars (5)
8. Not the brush Brummell used (5) —
9. but which he does (8)
15. Little Radicals? (8)
17. Rudolf was busy here (9)
18. Keen as heads lacking animation (4,4)
20. Night's hangover (7)
21. Shorten the crossing (7)
22. Not quite so fast (5)
23. Approaches (5)
24. He reverses a prohibition to peep (5)

7 JULY 1952

LONDON'S LAST TRAM

Across

1. Precise and gets most of the cordial (10)
6. This turn should have a twinkle in it (4)
10. Pigeons at sea (7)
11. Sundered hillock in a flood (7)
12. Mixed diets (5)
13. Guy's tenor (anag.) (9)
14. Changes of peals (5)
16. The tide turns among colleagues (9)
18. No port for armoured ships evidently (9)
19. This man is not necessarily partial (5)
21. He makes us each sly (9)
24. 'They——on you for weeks' (Dobson) (5)
25. His subjects were a lot of croakers (4, 3)
26. The umpire should know about such an account (7)
27. Time changes for the East Anglian river (4)
28. It was 'older than the centuries; older than the d'Urbervilles' (10)

Down

1. Examine in South America, Sarah (7)
2. Discomfort of Miss Procter's organist (3, 2, 4)
3. Nymph's request, having become an author (5)
4. Answer from Meredith embodied in a title (5)
5. Out! Sad end, and caused surprise (9)
7. Bridge of cricket (5)
8. 'Earth's——for whole centuries of folly, noise and sin' (Browning) (7)
9. Dress among the Parcae (8)
15. Chat less (anag.) (8)
16. It stimulated the emotions of Lorenzo and Jessica— and many others! (9)
17. The dowry turns up and might become modern (9)
18. Fly round the cabs (7)
20. 'Officious, innocent, ——' (Johnson) (7)
22. The Spanish gentleman (5)
23. Three points about an alternative (5)
24. Water on water which isn't (5)

29 MAY 1953

EVEREST CONQUERED: HILLARY AND TENZING REACH THE SUMMIT

Across

1, 10. The sort that leads to acts? (9,8)
11. What to do in musical chairs (4,1,4)
12. Stanley didn't find Livingstone here but you can (8)
13. Amazon in a dream (9)
14. It's quiet just before the race (8)
15. Sinful in a converted Red and lethal (9)
22. Tripping along (9)
23. There's a human lot in here (8)
24. All arm now in defence work (5,4)
25. One's only a second saying this (5,3)
26. A false friend of Pistol (9)
27. Is the school principal long-suffering? (8)
28. It's often on parade (9)

Down

2. About broken ideals as understood (8)
3. Little grouse, by the sound of them (8)
4. Atlantic liners are often so rude (8)
5. Roomy buildings (9,6)
6. Some show of reluctance in a novel hero (7)
7. Alice by name (7)
8. Feel the absence of Euripides's hero (7)
9. 'Round many western——have I been' (Keats) (7)
16. A mean mule in a place of learning (8)
17. Not the up express (4,4)
18. Not yet out of hand, perhaps (8)
19. A completely painful display? (7)
20. O, it's Othello's (7)
21. 'The folding ——s of the east' (Thompson) (7)
22. A dancing turn, but not on the halls (7)

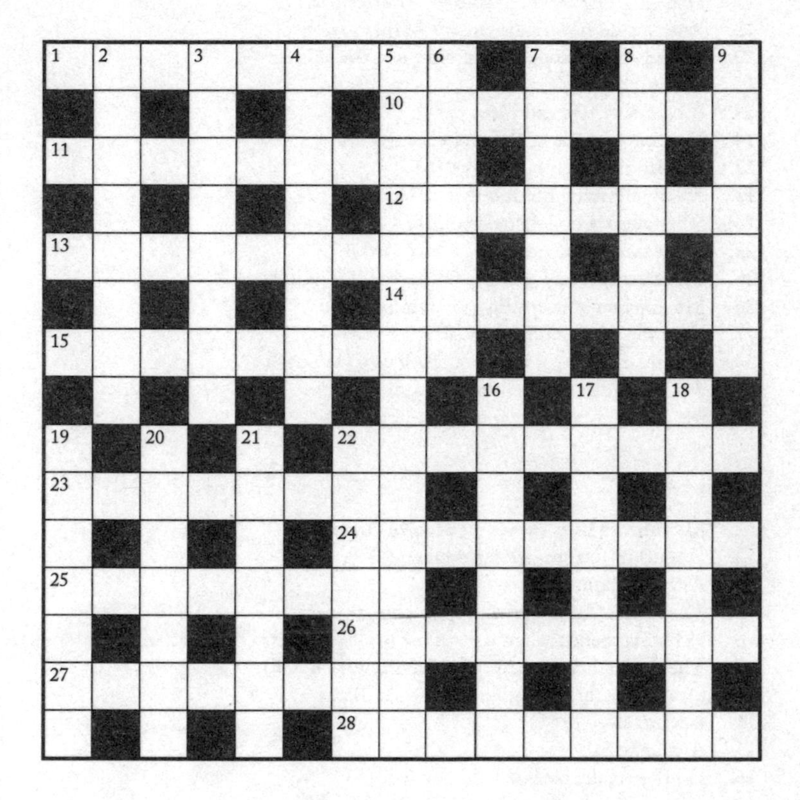

3 APRIL 1954

OXFORD WIN 100TH BOAT RACE

Across

1. Downing Street when women govern? (9, 4)
8. Amy, a glad new make-up, it's brainy (8)
9. It might make some impression initially (6)
12. Ground rice (4)
13. A company join the Fleet (5)
14. Nothing is made of this material (4)
17. Medico in the river is active (6)
18. Finally between the sheets and blown up (7)
20. Silly fellow who jolts relations (7)
22. The voice of the catfish or a bird? (6)
25. 'The thin harvest waves its withered——' (Crabbe) (4)
26. Much paper concerning a manuscript (5)
27. Dare the goddess change? (4)
30. 'The man had——the thing he loved' (Wilde) (6)
31. Seaman's idea of when to get wed? (8)
32. Made by rascals who vote twice? (6,7)

Down

2. 'My brother he is in——' (*Twelfth Night*) (7)
3. It leads to fortune properly taken (4)
4. A colic mixture (6)
5. The king of beasts provides his own dinner (4)
6. What happened when the nudist went to court? (7)
7. The brief story of pottery is electrifying (4, 3, 5)
10. Swallow a nip for snubbing (4, 4, 1, 3)
11. Keys to sleep in (5)
15. A chancy fish (5)
16. Do they really please as demanded? (5)
19. It might be displayed by Lear's daughter (5)
21. Strange turn before getting unfit comes to nothing (7)
23. The lock seems to be dead and cold (7)
24. Spoil the appearance of a little devil (6)
28. 'I'll set a bank of rue, sour——of grace' (*Richard II*) (4)
29. It controls the course of the wood (4)

1 2 3 4 5 6 7 8 9 10 11 12 13 14 15 16 17 18 19 20 21 22 23 24 25 26 27 28 29 30 31 32

9 MAY 1955

WEST GERMANY ACCEPTED INTO NATO

Across

1. Plate with which to dig in? (8)
5. Quick! Make a poster! (6)
9. Not the one that was won on the playing fields of Eton (8)
10. Hunger results when a tailor goes short of fish (6)
12. One gets a north-east touch after October, it's the hydrocarbon (6)
13. 'I taste no —— in boiled and roast' (Sydney Smith) (8)
15. Anything but the bowling that won the Leeds test (4,3,5)
18. Does he give one twenty-six cards? (6,6)
23. What's left? That's right (8)
24. Gum, Sir, is what the old bird's made of (6)
26. Jeer,—Who? That'll make one cry (6)
27. Don't be so tame (8)
28. 'Live a coward in thine own——' (*Macbeth*) (6)
29. The little more and how much (often) it is (2,6)

Down

1. 'I stood —— upon a little hill' (Keats) (6)
2. It goes into twenty which doesn't start (6)
3. Where 'we left him alone with his glory' (7)
4. The officer confuses one and ten (4)
6. A threesome in real circumstances requires further test (7)
7. It would change to rivers (8)
8. Superior part of the umpire's task is to be this (8)
11. Legislation for the chiropodist? (4,3)
14. Must Ida appear in it? (7)
16. Able to get round Dora, so charming! (8)
17. Fail to reach the crease and cause dearth (3,5)
19. There's nothing after the doctor in the lane but a robber (7)
20. A mineral from Ireland it seems (7)
21. Time somebody paid a subscription (6)
22. The constant nymph from Numa's point of view (6)
25. 'I know not where is that Promethean——' (*Othello*) (4)

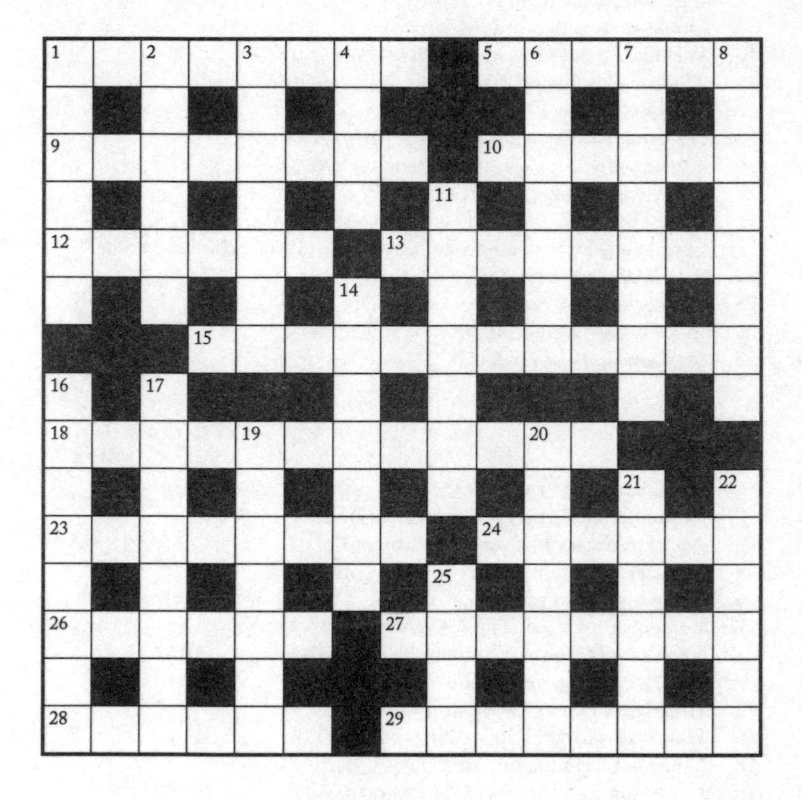

26 JULY 1956

NASSER ANNOUNCES NATIONALIZATION OF SUEZ CANAL

Across

1. It's woful, made to an eyebrow (6)
4. On pastry it is returned by saints (8)
10. Wherever it goes it is not so dusty (9)
11. Three crowns in one (5)
12. Shaw's Ramsden (7)
13. His horse was Bayard (7)
14. A temporary stoppage that goes on for ever (9, 5)
17. But there's nothing new in all this (7, 7)
21. Little brother to a rebel? That's the stuff (7)
22. 'O what a fall was there my countrymen!' said the returned traveller (7)
24. A lady of the sonnets (5)
25. Twenty shillings for the pound, perhaps (3, 6)
26. In every fifty there's 150 first (8)
27. Sir Thomas More's hall (6)

Down

1. A shady area in New York (6)
2. So our definite article is feminine in France (5)
3. Atmospherically it is very exhausting (7)
5. Matches or men or politico-social organizations (14)
6. Large enough to swing a cat in it (7)
7. But a quart of it won't go into a pint pot (5, 4)
8. They are not, however, responsible for the boiling surf (8)
9. Loungers' defensive attitude (5, 2, 3, 4)
15. Largely common robbery, as it were (9)
16. Hundreds surround the makings of a broil (8)
18. Come out from the manatee (7)
19. 'Let Nature be your——' (Wordsworth) (7)
20. The one vehicle welcomed on the roads (6)
23. The child-wife's successor (5)

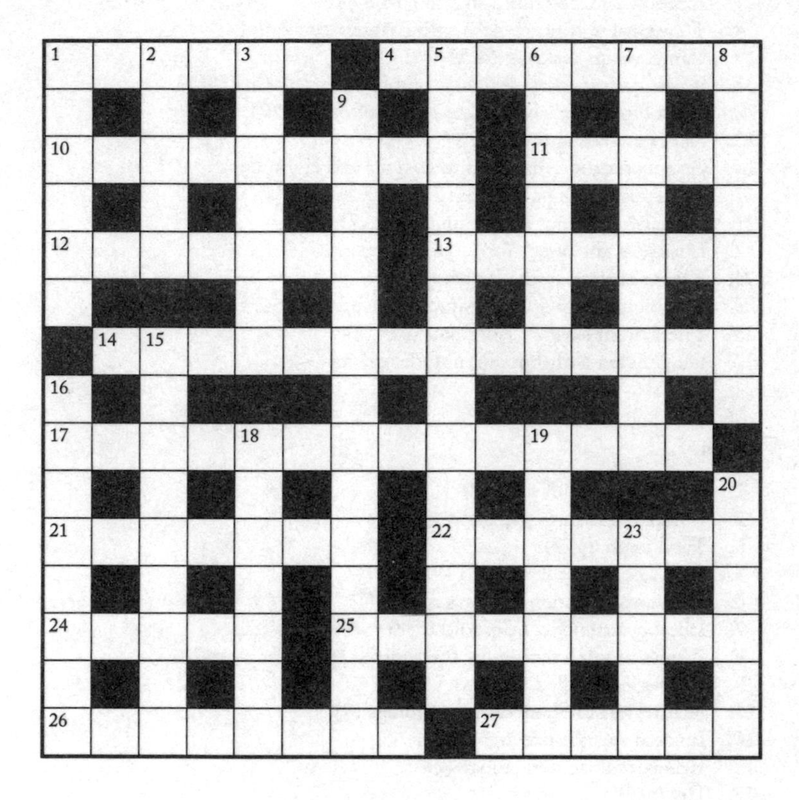

10 JANUARY 1957

HAROLD MACMILLAN BECOMES PRIME MINISTER

Across

1. 'A fellow almost damn'd in a fair wife' (6)
4. Though sick at heart, he is otherwise painstaking (8)
10. Can cowslips make it? (4,5)
11. It is so full of artless jealousy, said Hamlet's mother (5)
12. With him possession is nine points of the law (7)
13. Anger at getting the bird? (7)
14. Communication that used to cost six and eightpence (6,2,3,3)
17. Their rustling is not intended to be heard (6,8)
21. For sale? Well, not in working order (7)
22. Is close to the bone (7)
24. Reached by car in the North (5)
25. The humiliation of being among the bargain-hunters? (9)
26. The kind of sky the fisherman likes (8)
27. Football team of thirteen, not eleven? (6)

Down

1. A coming man of song (8)
2. It makes a hash of the mails (5)
3. Tend to go up (7)
5. As a rule it is pedestrian (14)
6. Her transformation can be genuine (7)
7. It's only a rumour, we're told (5,4)
8. A note in safe keeping for the surgeon (6)
9. Kansas is so-called (9,5)
15. Marine girl in Siamese surroundings (9)
16. It could suit the fire-fighter (8)
18. Rabelais's imaginary abbey (7)
19. Grave (7)
20. A race of twisters, so to speak (6)
23. 'Greet the unseen with a ——' (Browning) (5)

4 JANUARY 1958

EXPLORER EDMUND HILLARY REACHES SOUTH POLE

Across

1. A suggestion of wire-pulling at Delphi (4, 3, 6)
9. Begins radio for the Unfinished (4, 5)
10. 'Find no —— ter de golden gate?' (Harris) (5)
11. Conclude? No, that would be hellish! (5)
12. The Italian radical is rather stingy (9)
13. A specialist in puffs (7)
15. But he didn't sing 'They'll never believe me' (7)
17. The more confused it is (7)
19. Gray's crowd borrowed by Hardy (7)
21. Such a trying fellow! (9)
23. How December was nighted by Keats (5)
24. 'The —— lingers and sings' (Stevenson) (5)
25. Impossible contest for hens, even on the track (5, 4)
26. Stop in a crater (anag.) (13)

Down

2. Where to get a stone like 1958 (3, 2, 4)
3. One might look for him in Lusaka first (5)
4. He leads the Jollies, it's finished (7)
5. Dramatic victim of wet clothes (7)
6. Noah's last question before going into liquidation? (3, 6)
7. When to see the alligator? (5)
8. They don't always travel at a snail's pace (6)
9. How to throw the gin about (5)
14. Tranquillizer equal, for example, to mixed fibre (9)
16. Retain tin for travelling (9)
17. That lets us out of the contest (6)
18. Bad melody making one quite feverish (7)
19. 'This guest of summer, the temple-haunting ——' (*Macbeth*) (7)
20. Too much Cheddar? (5)
22. Conrad's dog was it? (5)
23. The same Japanese coin enjoying seniority (5)

1 2 3 4 5 6 7 8 9 10 11 12 13 14 15 16 17 18 19 20 21 22 23 24 25 26

1 JANUARY 1959

REBEL ARMY DRIVES OUT CUBAN DICTATOR BATISTA

JANE CARTON
Editor of The Times Crossword
1960–1965

On Carton's death in 1960 his wife, Jane, who had been contributing puzzles and helping with the editing for some years, took over. She had a pretty turn of wit – '*The greater snowdrop (9)*' and '*Foreign entanglements (9)*' [AVALANCHE and SPAGHETTI] – but her chief concern was always to check every possible fact; one must be certain that the solver could not write and say, 'I think this is unfair'.

John Grant, 1990

My task was greatly alleviated by the numerous contributions from those experts in their craft, Adrian Bell and my predecessor, Jane Carton, who had taken over the editorship from her husband on his death in 1960 and who gave me constant advice and assistance until her own sad death in 1971. If the reputation of *The Times* Crossword has been maintained since the death of Ronald Carton, this is due to a very great extent to Jane Carton and her devotion to the task of producing the best possible crosswords and of passing on to her neophyte successor the traditions so long created and developed by her husband and herself.

Edmund Akenhead, 1985

EDMUND AKENHEAD
Editor of The Times Crossword
1965–1983

Progression of The Times Crossword

The tendency, as I see it, has been towards getting more into the clues and to increase the proportion of 'double clues'. Not every clue provides two routes to the answer, the quotation clue (once much commoner in *Times* Crosswords than it is today) being one with only one route, but there are today many more 'build-up' clues than there were in the early days, pointing not only to the meaning of the word but showing how the word can be constructed. The devices used as bricks in this building-up process have tended to multiply and the patient solver is expected to know that 'direction', 'point' or 'quarter' in a clue is likely to indicate N, E, S or W, and 'note' can mean any letter from A to G or perhaps a note in the tonic sol-fa (do, re, me, etc.). Solvers are also expected to know the chemical abbreviations used for some of the better-known elements, such as Ag for silver, Fe for iron and Cu for copper, and to have knowledge of the definite and indefinite articles and other very simple words in French, German, Italian and Spanish (even Russian entered into a clue for OUIDA in the 1978 Championship Final).

A simple word like 'it' in a clue could mean 'Italian' (vermouth) or 'SA' (sex appeal) or vice versa, while 'of course' could mean 'naturally' or it could refer to golf-course, a race-track, a series of lectures or part of a meal. There are innumerable tricks of the trade which solvers will learn with experience. In particular, a solver must know the Roman numerals, with 'many' often meaning L, C, D or M; and must be prepared to translate a clue into Roman numerals, such as the clue 'L,000 in 1,200' for 'Marylebone' which, as every cricketer knows, is the 'M' in 'MCC.'

Edmund Akenhead, 1980

I am sorry if the more gifted solvers find the crossword too easy, but there has been no attempt to make it easier than it was, and it is thought that to make the puzzle noticeably harder would frustrate more solvers than it would please. It is easy enough to concoct really difficult clues but those who hunger after these will have to wait for the Eliminator Puzzle. If nevertheless a reader remains baffled by a clue in an ordinary *Times* Crossword and writes to me with a stamped addressed envelope for reply I shall always be glad to send the explanation.

Edmund Akenhead, 1983

The style of the crossword today owes much to Edmund Akenhead, who took over as editor from Jane Carton in 1965. As a life-long member of the Magic Circle, he felt that the cryptic crossword compiler has much in common with the conjurer, since it is his constant aim to misdirect the solver by mental sleight of hand. He was involved in two major developments, *The Times* Crossword

Championship and the Jumbo Puzzle, which he invented.

The Jumbo puzzles, which Akenhead started in *The Times* in 1970, were well described on the occasion of Akenhead's retirement in 1983 by Roy Dean, the retired diplomat who won the first *Times* Championship: 'What elephantine elegance, what breadth of erudition, what excitement, as the solver is led on from Shakespeare to Shaw, from the Bible to Brewer, from Ancient Greece to modern science, until the onset of writer's cramp forces the pen from his fingers. How fitting that the name of Akenhead can be clued as "A knowledge master" et in memoriam suam.'

John Grant, 1990

Letter to Edmund Akenhead as Editor of Times Crossword 1967

Dear Editor — In 1963 I moved to Westcliff-on-Sea in Essex in order to join the staff of Westcliff High School for Boys. In those days staff did have time for recreation, during the morning break and the lunch-hour. Some played shove-halfpenny, others including myself, did *The Times* Crossword. The 'star' solver was Alfred Bately, the Head of Maths, who had been at the school since 1928. He filled in the answers and allowed the rest of us to make an occasional contribution.

In July 1967 Alfred was due to retire. One of my colleagues wrote to the Crossword Editor of *The Times* to ask if it would be possible to include in the crossword of the day of his departure an appropriate clue. The reply came back that the crossword was certainly not the place for passing on personal messages!

On the last day of the Summer Term – probably about July 21st – before Alfred appeared, some of us started doing the crossword. If I remember rightly, One Across produced the answer Good-bye Mr Chips and I think another answer was Alfred. It rapidly became clear to us that the Crossword Editor was not as stony-hearted as his letter had led us to believe. A virgin copy of *The Times* was retrieved from the school library and it was left to Alfred to decode the messages. His delight was immense and, of course, that copy of *The Times* left with him.

Yours sincerely,
John D. Hart

THE SIXTIES

Across

1. You should spot this! (8)
5. 'I have —— much, Cynara! gone with the wind' (Dowson) (6)
9. Fishermen's littoral activities? (8)
10. Blamed for the uproar here (6)
12. The poet had obviously become it when he wrote 'I remember' (7)
13. But at this place should one not first be up? (7)
14. Not quite what Shakespeare meant by sea-maids (12)
17. 'Save thine —— oil, Macassar!' (Byron) (12)
22. Eyed (7)
23. Jonson's Revel Maid perhaps (7)
24. Confection that vanishes like lightning? (6)
25. Swine encased in fat (8)
26. 'Until Thine azure —— of the spring shall blow Her clarion' (Shelley) (6)
27. Costumes for mermaids? (8)

Down

1. Apothecaries' notes (6)
2. Chain seen in intricate navigation (6)
3. Warning in a gazebo (4,3)
4. What laundresses do on the line is somewhat deflating (4,4,1,3)
6. Time for a change—more than time! (7)
7. Prize dog salve in a pot (4,4)
8. Burns's hero, unplaced, takes a chance (8)
11. The old man dined in state (12)
15. Flowers created by the embroiderer? (8)
16. Lightweights make difficulties (8)
18. People who got a nip from the old bird (7)
19. It is drawn in exaggeration (7)
20. Dr Johnson's pen-friend (6)
21. Unworthy chap, Pluto (6)

20 JULY 1960

CEYLON ELECTS WORLD'S FIRST WOMAN PM

Across

1. Where a Spaniard might expect to get the sack (6)
4. Wrongdoer tender about the behind (8)
10. In Trent beside the Wye (7)
11. To a writer one more child? (7)
12. Feast that gives rise to sore heads? (4, 6)
13. Mars produces them (4)
15. In a small quantity I'd find little taste (7)
17. Big steamer from voluntary donations (7)
19. Necessary to the preparation of fish teas? (7)
21. Servicemen's dining room in a city of Sicily (7)
23. Coastal cover for 13 (4)
24. Telepathic inspirations? (10)
27. It's a matter of luck that Tarka is in (7)
28. Canadian Lakeland (7)
29. Wild warrior to denude a Channel Isle (8)
30. Decoration of the fridge? (6)

Down

1. Not that the city is of this (4, 5)
2. Russian footballers for a generation (7)
3. Fat is a handicap to climbing this (6, 4)
5. A runner gets the whip in Rome (9)
6. They never met at Micawber's (4)
7. 'As much as I —— ! Why, that's the lady' (*M. of V.*) (7)
8. They can make holes in householders' pockets (5)
9. A Dickensian without his pea-jacket (4)
14. Bay salt or not? (10)
16. Which prevails if this ship meets breakers? (9)
18. Lathery alternative to 1 down? (9)
20. He offers to guide you when you are backing (7)
22. Metrical topsy-turvy (7)
23. Cable-maker (5)
25. Club used on the lawn (4)
26. Organized parties going by air (4)

20 JANUARY 1961

JOHN F. KENNEDY SWORN IN AS PRESIDENT

Across

1. The meat's growing whiskers! (6, 4)
6. Doll Tearsheet was said to be sick of one (4)
10. She gets to New York at speed (5)
11. It's not for jottings (9)
12. Try Hay's Lido for a change (8)
13. Gives out like certain namesakes (6)
15. Horses in hard case (4)
16, 17. Standard 14 lb. as laid down (9)
20. Inward type of woman (5)
21. Singularly chancy, but in the plural might be seen through (4)
22. Cottontail (4)
24. Clumsy fingers (6)
26. Random author, clinker-builder, pickler (8)
29. Thoughtful? Let her not count her chickens yet (6, 3)
30. Each of these counts as one although it looks like ten (5)
31. The muster includes these (4)
32. Routes that become roundabout (10)

Down

1. Monsieur takes a bite of lunch (5)
2. Hence counsels' refreshers? (6, 3)
3. Neat coat (2-4)
4. Preserve Little Florence in sugar? (5, 5)
5. Grain that might dry hops (4)
7. Green and red and may be pied (5)
8. Where Pegasus was fledged? Sheer illusion! (5-4)
9. Pacify a legume-stuffed monkey (7)
14. A green stem contracts (10)
15. Security man in the National Gallery (9)
18. Grampus, he's taken up art—music in fact (9)
19. Rotund philanthropist in a green jacket? (7)
23. A hundred and fifty always have brains (6)
25. Stevenson lived here (5)
27. More jobs for Cowper? (5)
28. Trout, lady? (4)

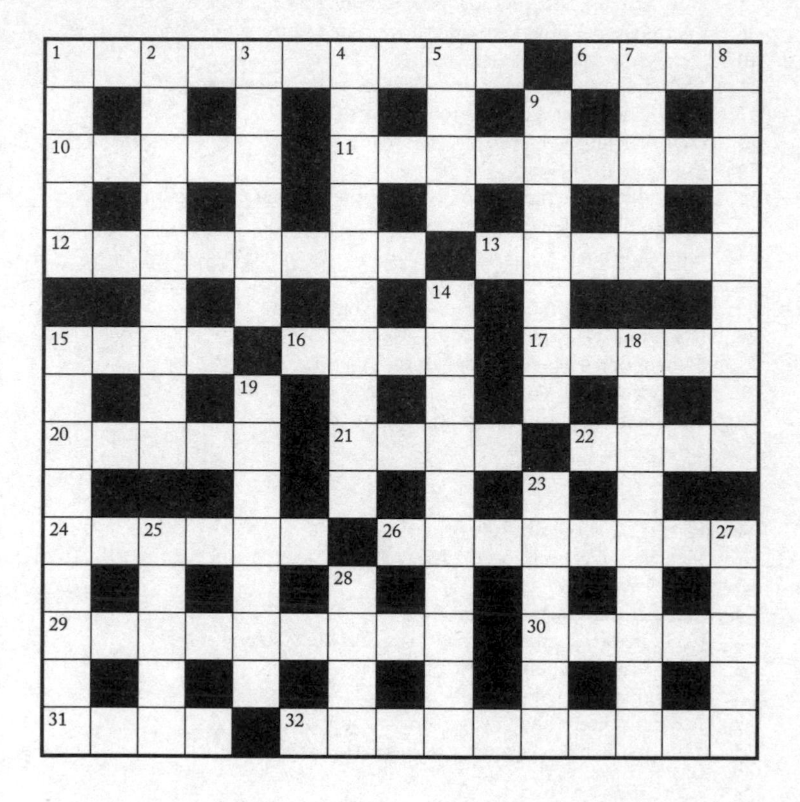

26 APRIL 1962

FIRST US ROCKET LANDS ON MOON

Across

1. How a doctor describes his partner? One may hold a gun (8)
5. The minimum of money for a Buckinghamshire saint (6)
10. He's in the wars (9)
11. They measure the fluctuating fortunes of the class struggle (5)
12. Paper that's always getting into scrapes (5)
13. How many tiny soft hairs are needed to send a man to the moon? (5,4)
14. Embraces the boots? (7)
16. Examples of the rigid stand of the French in matters of grain (6)
19. Refuses to be daunted by people on the warpath (6)
21. Kind of name (7)
23. Lords and ladies stir a bird (4-5)
25. Tea by which he might be got fatally tight (5)
26. Peter to be principal boy? (5)
27. State of one who is weary of Burns's women? (9)
28. Longer stop (6)
29. Anything but pushful men of business (8)

Down

1. Having a fowl squint? (4-4)
2. Pickwickian convalescent? (3, 6)
3. Is table-talk so mouthed? (5)
4. Ten cars transported by spirit (7)
6. Consulted by some who wish to change their stations (4-5)
7. Miss Rome is among the stars (5)
8. Sol is first seen with the rebels (6)
9. Parades conceitedly, having plenty of support (6)
15. This past human reckoning was the Alph riverain (9)
17. Pub that goes with a job? (4,5)
18. They go by water (8)
20. Girls who look ahead (6)
21. Rummy type of basket from abroad (7)
22. Drank all the worst beer? (6)
24. Two books of supreme importance (5)
25. Sea-fish from Bucks (5)

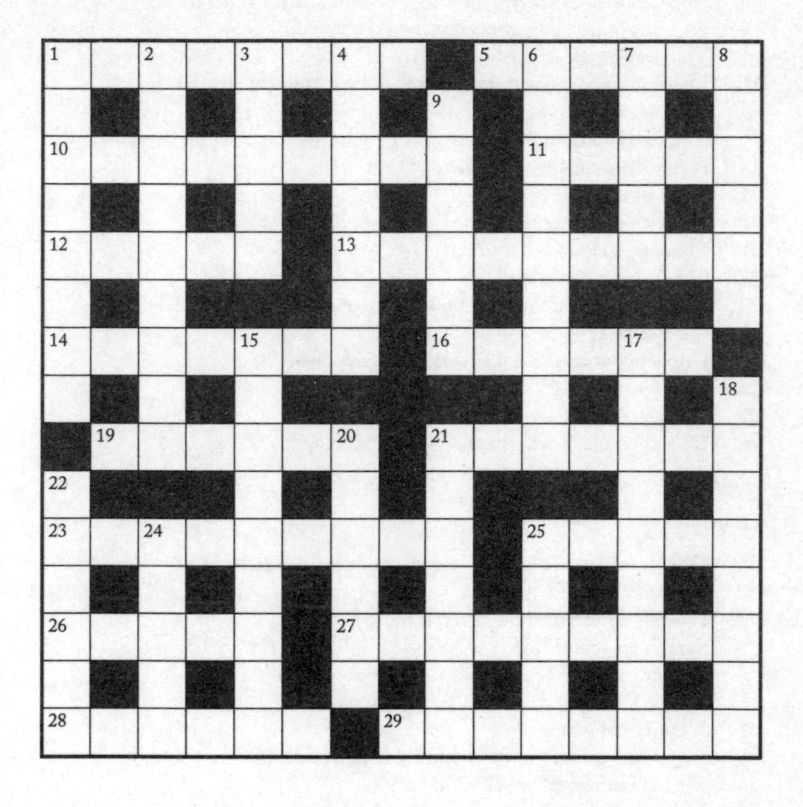

14 JANUARY 1963

FRENCH VETO BRITAIN'S EEC BID

Across

1. The Chairman's preference is no secret with this (7, 4)
7. '—— makes rattling good history' (Hardy) (3)
9. Wander alongside this in Lakeland (5)
10. Figuratively speaking, they shouldn't be mixed (9)
11. Maize (7)
12. The royal leg? (4-3)
14. Stevenson's mistress was the open sort (4)
15. A bit throaty (9)
19. Whence to expect news for the oenophilist? (4-5)
20. Spooner makes such a to-do (4)
22. One is sorry to do it (7)
23. Beach provides point of no return for one who has imbibed too freely (7)
24. Unpoetic writing but pleasing; do you follow? (9)
26. Two for coloured (5)
27. Up the boys! (3)
28. Certainly not Noah's system of accountancy (6, 5)

Down

1. Double-edged appeal for supplies from the modeller (8)
2. A stickler for rest-days (11)
3. Peaceful in intent though wrathful at first (6)
4. Sarah's protectors (5)
5. Border country where trews only are permissible? (9)
6. Next open the index (8)
7. Identity requested (3)
8. Siren can't be said to be lacklustre in this form (5)
13. Mr Palliser's royal appellation (11)
16. The pantomime dog (9)
17. Winds and streams (8)
18. The street of Denis Mackail (8)
21. Simon's remedy (6)
22. Reject it. What? The little bird (5)
23. The stuff of 1 down (5)
25. In possession, one must admit (3)

12 JUNE 1964

NELSON MANDELA JAILED FOR LIFE

Across

1. It could give a fair amount of pleasure—or pain (10)
6. A Red let off (4)
10. For the protection of motorists' pupils? (7)
11. Explore caves to find the birds (7)
12. Would a coach tour be a busman's holiday for him? (5)
13. The punishment that fits a major crime? (9)
14. Buttons swallows a bit of food with hesitation (9)
17. But it may mean everything to an actor (4)
20. A man from the New World (4)
21. What the dishonest reporter might do? (4,5)
24. Is the peach their favourite fruit? (9)
26. Who gets the bird? He does, for cash (5)
28. Delay in giving the criminal his due? (4,3)
29. Material to a loser, doubtless (7)
30. Continually in a daydream (4)
31. Shakespearian robin (10)

Down

1. 'Her —— and sounds; dreams happy as her day' (Brooke) (6)
2. Gin to be obtained at the bar (5)
3. Speed in a mixed dance in an urban setting (8)
4. They are not necessarily scenes of low life (5)
5. Map change that affects part of France (9)
7. One way to make crackling (9)
8. The most improvident can afford to pay them (8)
9. Does it give the directors food for thought? (5)
15. Old French standard (9)
16. It's illuminating to the following (4-5)
18. 'We are seven' (8)
19. Frank's condition (8)
22. Insular, and sound as a bell (5)
23. Byron's Boatswain, for example? (6)
25. Broadcaster in 'Gardening Club'? (5)
27. A word of all-embracing significance (5)

18 JUNE 1965

BILL INTRODUCED ON DRINKING AND DRIVING

Across

1. Three legs under four legs, neatly put (7, 5)
9. Fool, that's nothing to crow over, on the contrary (9)
10. The ears he leaves are from the eyes (5)
11. State of exaltation we get into on entering a store (6)
12. 'Be bloody, bold, and ——' (*Macbeth*) (8)
13. Golden mink? That would create a sensation (6)
15. Prevalence of money (8)
18. A fell old man (8)
19. If you change your mac, Ida, you'll be in the nude (6)
21. Vinous, and what a sketch! (8)
23. An incarnation (6)
26. Noted totem (5)
27. What a row it makes in London and anywhere (9)
28. What the potter did for haute couture? (7,5)

Down

1. Chieftain o' the pudding race (7)
2. That's the colour of our inn (5)
3. Abyssinian prince hiding in the lounge? To that extent (2,2,3,2)
4. This provides the stop in a sentence (4)
5. Just picture them all still! (8)
6. Excel at a fête champêtre (5)
7. Toothy affectation (7)
8. Hood's brother planted one, he remembered (8)
14. Make off with a gem, the vagabond (8)
16. Fiery sunset, cut, and do the darkroom work again? (9)
17. Merriment goes on all day this way, it is said (8)
18. Smugglers' sentry? A rough old sort (7)
20. A Welsh husband (7)
22. Go out in front of the gunners, not I, that would be more than one bargained for (5)
24. The painter from the Cyclades (5)
25. Oh to rise to the purple! (4)

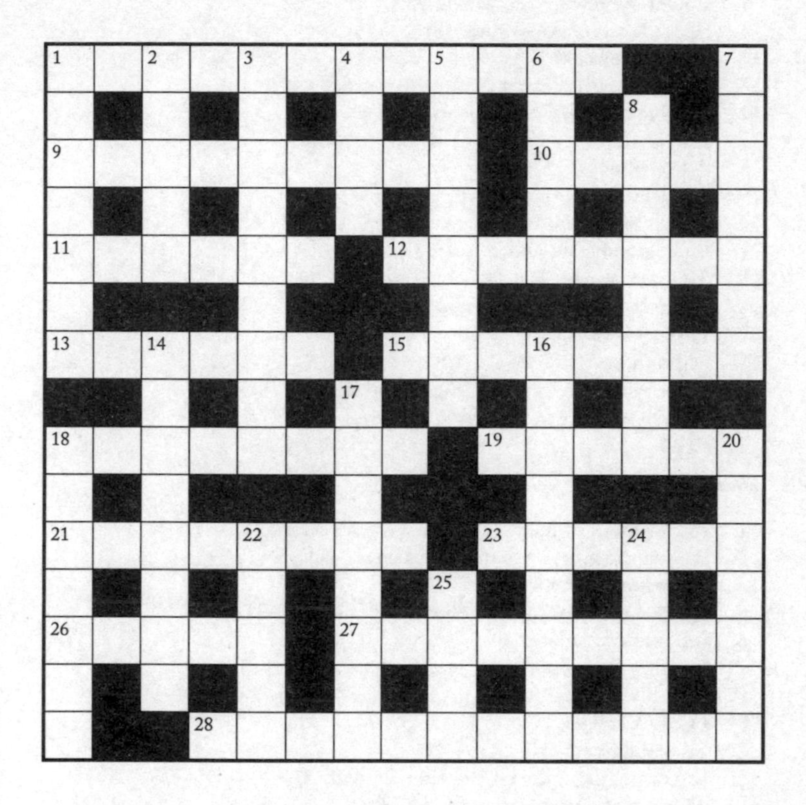

20 OCTOBER 1966

GEORGE BLAKE ESCAPES FROM WORMWOOD SCRUBS

See 'A Visit from MI5' on page 150

Across

1. Cauldron brew for the wedding? (6)
4. Add a touch of Angostura? (8)
10. The palace walk? (7)
11. The VIP can't make it (7)
12. Laws to contain TNT menaces (10)
13. A light pistol (4)
15. A live wire? (7)
17. The jelly-fish with the stony glance? (7)
19. Obliterate—with water, presumably (7)
21. Reprehensible falsehood heard from cephalopods (7)
23. 'The very word is like a ——' (Keats) (4)
24. Look a gift-horse in the mouth as donors might? (10)
27. Poet's flower (7)
28. Milton Grove (7)
29. Elder statesmen of the old world and the new (8)
30. It's no good, the net return in this (6)

Down

1. And without so much as a thank-you for Keats! (5, 4)
2. It's just showing off to drop eggs on a good man (7)
3. But *generally* senior to a major (10)
5. Quick-march for this member of the militia (6-3)
6. Just jot down a letter (4)
7. Are they for writing drug prescriptions? (7)
8. Like Blake's rural pen? (5)
9. Friendly address (4)
14. Sit in judgment (10)
16. Inspector Alexander on the old railway (3-6)
18. The way of a poetic tenor? Odd! (9)
20. Tug-of-war competitor in the train (7)
22. Edomite (7)
23. Dandies are in the money in USA (5)
25. What a change in the weather! (4)
26. 'It is the little —— within the lute' (Tennyson) (4)

5 JUNE 1967

ISRAEL LAUNCHES WAR ON ARAB STATES

Across

1. Making excuses about certain dissipations, perhaps (9)
6. Cutting too high? (5)
9, 10. King takes car trip with dramatist and poet (7,7)
11. Spots the animals? (5)
12. S. African without keenness for battle (9)
13. Dickensian sees another in a back-street (8)
15. Dull poet retires (4)
19. Wander through Provence? (4)
20. Bird gets some grain (8)
23. Perhaps driving people from the border? (9)
24. Custom makes us laugh a little (5)
26. Child writes notes? (7)
27. Twelve ducks after one? What a lot! (7)
28. Quietly takes late irregulars into the fold (5)
29. Feature of precipice in Kent? (9)

Down

1. Fairy encountered queen by boundary (9)
2. Surpass forty—to speak classically (5)
3. Such froth from Dolly! (4-4)
4. Artist has lots of food—vegetables (8)
5. Understand we have about up to a month to withdraw (6)
6. A ship to make one's mouth water? (6)
7. Gives one a brush, being untidy, in Derbyshire (9)
8. Might follow horse? (5)
14. Make statement on hoarding? (9)
16. Singers take it with a single in places of refreshment (9)
17, 18. Single high-born visitor to Baker Street? (3,5,8)
21. Where people live and play? (6)
22. It's a 5s. error, in some views (6)
23. Deeply afflicted the TUC, apparently (3,2)
25. 'The —— hath paced into the hall' (Coleridge) (5)

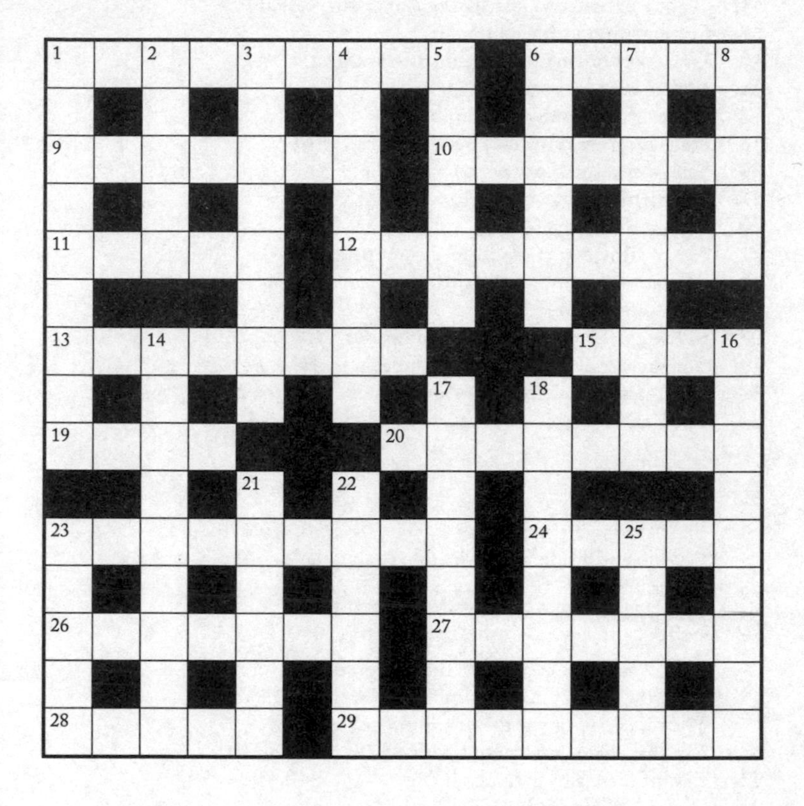

4 APRIL 1968

MARTIN LUTHER KING SHOT DEAD

Across

1. Go one better than just having skill, Brown! (10)
6. Combination of Frenchmen (4)
10. Poetic sort of rhyme to incur disaster (5)
11. Yankee island cocktail (9)
12. Regrets for the uncertain present (7)
13. He is in a rare state, this hospital founder (6)
16. 'Vain pomp and glory of the world, I —— ye' (*Henry VIII*) (4)
17. Weather warnings from Mons sector (5,5)
20. Ancients' trousers (10)
21. Noteworthy object of Gray's distant prospect (4)
23. Relative appearing in the part of a magnate (6)
25. Peter is maybe due for a breather (7)
28. In France the monsieur has a prayer for the scholar (9)
29. The more there are, the faster the boat is made (5)
30. Did Yeats plant these bean-rows in honour of the Muses? (4)
31. Their national spirit was expressed by Sibelius (10)

Down

1. The heart of the matter (4)
2. Detective of academic distinction (9)
3. Associated with spade work on the Strand (6)
4. Restrictive practice? (10)
5. The shade of 21 (4)
7. Being supple he gets under the foreign bed (5)
8. 'With thee —— I forget all time' (Milton) (10)
9. The remainder is for the equilibrist to keep (7)
14. Not that the dog finding it would be so dejected! (10)
15. Zest of the Ulster striptease? (6-4)
18. Out and ill at ease (3,2,4)
19. Whence to expect an assault by the chef? (7)
22. The word of the broadcaster (6)
24. Not that this classic appellation is confined to the distaff side! (5)
26. Fairy upsets one representative (4)
27. 'To what base —— we may return, Horatio!' (*Hamlet*) (4)

1		2		3		4		5		■	6	7		8
	■		■		■		■		■	9	■		■	
10					■	11								
	■		■		■		■		■		■		■	
■	12							■	13					
14	■		■		■		■	15	■		■	■	■	
16				■	17							18		
	■		■	19	■		■		■		■		■	
20										■	21			
	■	■	■		■		■		■	22	■		■	
23		24				■	25							■
	■		■		■	26	■		■		■		■	27
28									■	29				
	■		■		■		■		■		■		■	
30				■	31									

21 JULY 1969

AMERICA LANDS MAN ON THE MOON

THE SEVENTIES

Across

1. Rome rising to create the Italian Renaissance (12)
8. Name for a grass-widower? (7)
9. Sound chaps, the Egyptian peasants (7)
11. An entirely chilly greeting (3, 4)
12. I arrive here in a mess (7)
13. Coppers are after her in droves (5)
14. Needled, perhaps, but suffering no ill effects (9)
16. He supplies our daily needs (9)
19. Not a planned feature of a passing-out parade (5)
21. A den set in part of London (4, 3)
23. It has an absorbing interest for the penman (7)
24. Did this literary club take life too seriously? (7)
25. Florence's magnificent man (7)
26. A fortiori one cannot serve these ships (5-7)

Down

1. Pedestrian rose (7)
2. It's Sparta's turn for governors (7)
3. It requires a ruler, naturally, to provide this (5, 4)
4. Conclude that it's hell without a negative (5)
5. Make quick erratic line to the archdeacon (7)
6. They follow established lines (7)
7. Commuters who in the rush hour … (5-7)
10. … only have this space (8, 4)
15. A fly-by-night dances away from them (4-5)
17. Was Titipu's noble lord only half so spiteful? (7)
18. Mine hostess's fish (3-4)
19. Cause of widespread affliction when cures go awry (7)
20. Excursions enjoyed by the fielding side? (7)
22. That of Gerontius was noted (5)

22 JANUARY 1970

HEATHROW WELCOMES FIRST JUMBO JET

Across

1. Linen type of helmet (5)
4. Rhythmically footloose member of the jet set? (3-6)
9. End of martinet, confounded by egg-head (9)
10. Loves to devour a volume, mouldy though it is (5)
11. A row with the French tends to fester (6)
12. What backers of horses must expect? (8)
14. His houses are heavenly (10)
16. One's scared when it blows up (4)
19. He bring letters back (4)
20. Record sum made by Olympic athlete (10)
22. Old as original sin, say? (8)
23. A bit dicey with a crown (6)
26. To one side of Jack, a Biblical eyeful (5)
27. Put to bed, perhaps, I tend lamp (9)
28. Importance thrust on some, if not Malvolio (9)
29. In vulgar parlance it is not a blemish (5)

Down

1. How Puss may win his Boots? (9)
2. Stage for HMS Pinafore? (5)
3. Prized possession sounds of benefit to weavers of songs (8)
4. Shrew wanders in a wood (4)
5. These shares for choice? (10)
6. A river-horse in orbit? How way-out can you get? (6)
7. Annoyed on account of one bird … (9)
8. … fleeces others (5)
13. Oyster out of order in this case (10)
15. Lake where Hannibal broke up a thousand trainees? (9)
17. Shame! Don't believe it! (9)
18. Plentiful supply from British sailor and German worker (8)
21. Let me advise you on hair management (6)
22. In an RAF 1 *ac* 'quietly tinkled' understates things (5)
24. Is ye owner of single elephant (5)
25. Work one side of the stage with you and me (4)

This puzzle, used at the Edinburgh regional final of the Cutty Sark/Times Crossword Championship, was solved within 30 minutes by 6 out of 55 finalists.

9 AUGUST 1971

NORTHERN IRELAND ACTIVATES INTERNMENT LAW

Across

1. Strip tease imitation? (4-3)
5. It's real in the form of a cross (7)
9. Apparent cut-down (so expect a refund) (9)
10. Birds as a guide to the horses (5)
11. What Silvia would do in Rome at forty, say? (5)
12. It must be the 24 (9)
14. But it's a good lie, whatever the season (6,8)
17. As a sequence even I'd arrange to turn this (6,8)
21. Could the parson, for instance, be lying? (9)
23. Leave this reel for the fish (5)
24. The cash in hand? (5)
25. Too early, like the minority (9)
26. The fish to beat its victim (7)
27. The present radio release? (3,4)

Down

1. Worked on the books, also took first place (6)
2. Cape Kennedy's opening can provide joint cover (4-3)
3. Astronomical number the Italian brightened the company up with (9)
4. Game birds obstruct the hunter (3,3,5)
5. For some sob-sisters, a description? (3)
6. Singers on the way up (5)
7. Prepare to send the economic balloon up? (7)
8. Lear's daughter had one on a string (8)
13. Drivers causing a riot amid applause (11)
15. Incisive worker in World War I? (9)
16. The joiner who made Queen Mab's chariot (8)
18. Once a miner's piece of land, I do declare! (7)
19. Get one's opponent's at breaking-point in the game, say (7)
20. 'That unhoped ——, That men call age' (Brooke) (6)
22. What Roy early to rise can become (5)
25. Make regular journeys in the Strand? (3)

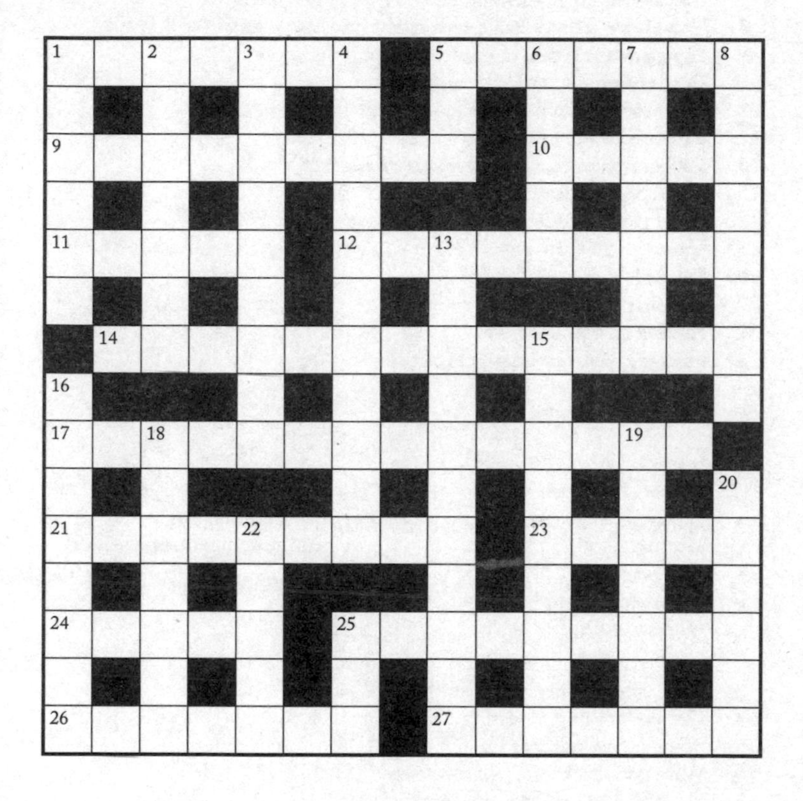

16 FEBRUARY 1972

MINERS' STRIKE TURNS OFF THE LIGHTS

Across

1. Occasioned no gentleman being out of employment (6)
5. How Judge Jeffreys dealt with twelve indecisive men? (4, 4)
9. Short passage recalls the smell—of midnight oil? (8)
10. False god around the service station (6)
11. Anguished cry in unprotected carriage (8)
12. Hunt about for a polecat (6)
13. Public tributes that nobody acknowledges (8)
15. To Dot—neckware (4)
17. Heart trouble ending in death? Hamlet wondered (4)
19. Plastered, but performed (8)
20. Smoked—smelt awful! (6)
21. Unburdens old magistrates—about £1 (8)
22. All that's left of order (6)
23. Offered to nurse a broken reed (8)
24. Historical movie (8)
25. Decide to alight (6)

Down

2. Short, short, long—the sound of Anna on the ski trail (8)
3. Dim, but dogged (8)
4. Apt description of Mycroff Holmes? (9)
5. Lehar ends tangle—changes opera (6, 3, 6)
6. Old boys readily spout to willing listeners (7)
7. Small-scale—not like the style of Pope's Homer (8)
8. Time of year when you'll get knotted, say? (8)
14. Drudges relish gin, getting squiffy (9)
15. Stone to press forward to get fish (8)
16. Wave goes back—helped on its way? (8)
17. Head broken and torn needs a sticker (8)
18. Blossom takes beer, maybe, in college dining-room (8)
19. Make a stage come-back (2-5)

26 MARCH 1973

STOCK EXCHANGE ADMITS WOMEN FOR FIRST TIME

Across

1. Workers added note about unwanted furniture (8)
9. He takes the stakes and makes childish complaint about one backer (8)
10. Fail to do something after an order (4)
11. Wister's work, features one of Thackeray's Americans (3, 9)
13. Author Laurence is back, we hear (6)
14. Unusual work in Milton, but not on this plant (8)
15. In favour of a smoother outline (7)
16. Enliven mount carrying foreign friend back (7)
20. Neat American poker hand (8)
22. Deduce that it needs pluck? (6)
23. German artist suggests the arrival of Spring (12)
25. Legislature appears in paper—endlessly (4)
26. Vagabond gets a railway union to return entrance money (8)
27. Redhead meeting irregular soldiers (8)

Down

2. Light on wild tree by Welsh town (8)
3. Prosaic affair—cricket side has to perform (6-2-4)
4. Heavenly anaesthetic—a brew of ale! (8)
5. Hundreds upset over his writing of divisions in the Church (7)
6. The Asian Doctor Long treated? (6)
7. Car of note isn't finished (4)
8. Woman is a beast about the tennis fixture (8)
12. Manhattan's Dutch-style town is now in Guyana (3,9)
15. Carried by Minstrel Boy to give to the sentry? (8)
17. Witch seen close to Gath settlement (5-3)
18. Isn't he a piano composer, or player? (8)
19. Vessel might be given letters in middle of crossing (7)
21. Composer of Beethoven's description? (6)
24. A number content to turn in early? (4)

1 2 3 4 5 6 7 8 9 10 11 12 13 14 15 16 17 18 19 20 21 22 23 24 25 26 27

17 JUNE 1974

IRA BOMBS PARLIAMENT

Across

1. Bloomer calls for, I trust, a revision in numbers (10)
6. Cover for the Admiral (4)
9. Deliveries to bodies of men which attract interest (10)
10. Soldier and Saint get the point (4)
12. Keeping September 3rd booking (12)
15. Flower—it may be confused with an acorn (9)
17. Could it be Melba who is so acclaimed? (5)
18. A beast? Right—no end of a swine (5)
19. To do a washing job many emulate Barnes's apple tree (5, 4)
20. West put in individual wood members as crossbars (12)
24. Been prostrate in a minor road, we hear (4)
25. Pigs do GCE? A new form of teaching (10)
26. How much work in Schönberg's music? (4)
27. Figures first in a branch of physics (10)

Down

1. Out of the question for a Scotsman at this time? (4)
2. The man she married (4)
3. Promises of jobs (12)
4. Sharp reverse in transport (5)
5. Complete sugar plant processing in a manner of speaking (9)
7. Inventor of banking system set up in a high place (10)
8. Causing an explosion by making appointment out of school (10)
11. Aunt Ena rocks crazily when quarrelsome (12)
13. One of fourteen herein that go the other way (6, 4)
14. Arranging possible accompaniment to which I perform (10)
16. Not fair for a postwar PM in the first place (9)
21. Cook in the right kiln (5)
22. Doubly an upstanding Parisienne? (4)
23. Such poisonous creatures have no right in the files (4)

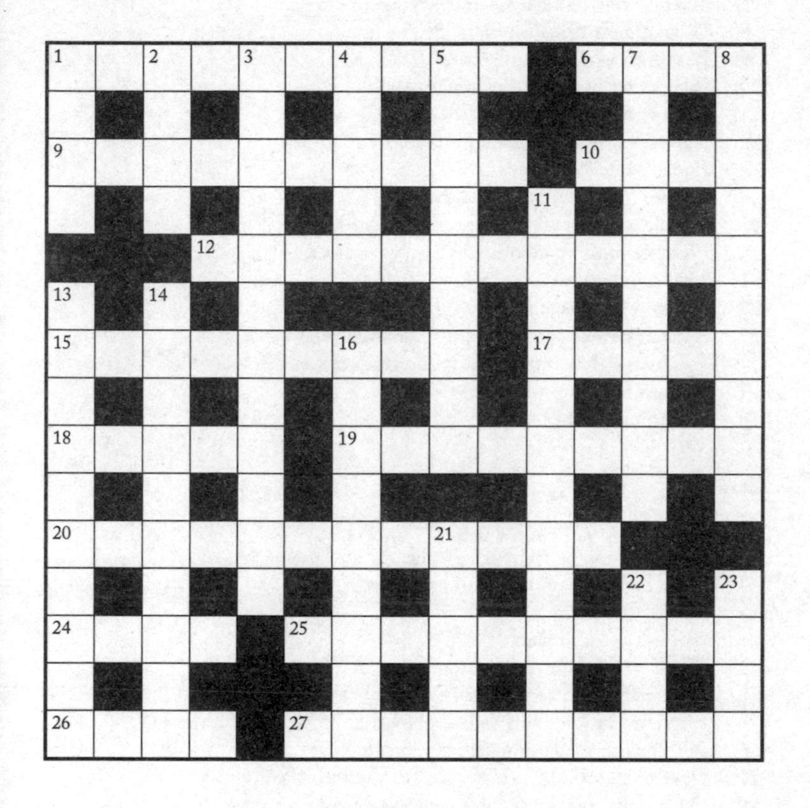

9 JUNE 1975

FIRST LIVE BROADCAST OF PARLIAMENT

Across

1. Having wine on board is outrageous (6)
5. What a monstrous waterspout! (8)
9. Downcast as one cast down (10)
10. Rich man, short of a shilling, may plunge (4)
11. Reg's neat trick may repel (8)
12. Kipling's ladies in transports (6)
13. Piper's bird? (4)
15. Workers love me, being so liberal (8)
18. Certain keys used by a fixer in a tizzy (4, 4)
19. Florence's flower produced on artist's return (4)
21. I ran into one (6)
23. Malvolio's sickness fatal to Narcissus (4-4)
25. It's the fate of Scandinavia to lack a navy (4)
26. Pompous dandy unpopular with cruise passengers? (5, 5)
27. Use ignition once more (8)
28. Bad communist press infuriates one sort of speculator (3, 3)

Down

2. Funny sort of fences! (5)
3. Despite its name it makes plagiarism an offence (9)
4. Silvia had their universal commendation (6)
5. Midas's parting gift? (6, 9)
6. Bad fish causing pain (8)
7. Times description, far from modern in 5 *dn* (5)
8. Is he irritable in company? (9)
14. It sounds an infernally tedious bloomer (could be a stinker) (9)
16. Put up with the two quarters permitted (9)
17. Gave press prominence to pass held with difficulty (8)
20. Once it wasn't cricket for a gentleman to be an actor (6)
22. Sounds bright and cheerful, the Prophet's follower (5)
24. Scientist from upper part of Africa? (5)

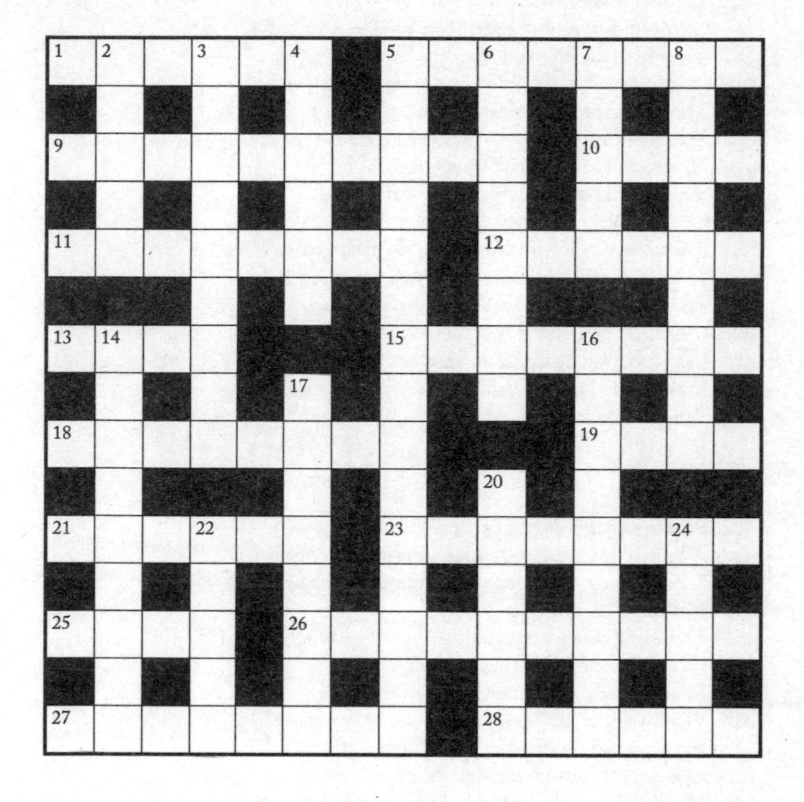

16 MARCH 1976

MR CALLAGHAN LIKELY SUCCESSOR AFTER SHOCK DECISION BY HAROLD WILSON TO RESIGN

Across

1. Shelter President's assassin (5)
4. One such flower mounted for Coventry exhibition (5,4)
9. It's not like Bertha to issue regular reports (6-3)
10. Classical quartet complete, returned home (5)
11. Record has to move slowly from left to right (6)
12. Sort of sitting for day-to-day business? (3-5)
14. He deposits vital liquid assets in bank (5,5)
16. When such parts function, we hear (4)
19. Cheese, with marts newly built in Amsterdam (4)
20. Instrumental in providing tea and rolls? (6-4)
22. In which soldiers appear in reversed stripes (8)
23. Thrown off ship, what? Go by air, man (6)
26. Come, Trojans, bring out transport for Paris (5)
27. Law-breaking in Central America, perhaps, the main disturbance (5,4)
28. Building up NHS? Yes, it's in need of change (9)
29. What this fish is, if not fresh (5)

Down

1. Beadle on working party's a noisy worker (6-3)
2. Admitted on Wednesday, needing treatment (5)
3. Schoolmen of high degree are impetuous fellows (8)
4. Not quite 12, but close (4)
5. The work, though unusual, contains nothing novel (10)
6. Guess what sort of drink Jonson craved (6)
7. Reptile needs a breather going up a hill (9)
8. Why, we hear, Brown's pal is cause of ferment (5)
13. Early proponent of world revolution (10)
15. Ape doesn't finish fruit, cracks a nut (5-4)
17. Member has whip-round—more soft-hearted than 19 (9)
18. Young things in the bar set loose (8)
21. Even Jacob was (6)
22. Uncle booked, initiating consumer backlash (5)
24. Blunt speaker's calling card? (5)
25. Bowled one as required—making use of this? (4)

This puzzle, used at the London B regional final of the Cutty Sark/Times National Crossword Championship, was solved within 30 minutes by 47 percent of the finalists.

16 AUGUST 1977

ROCK AND ROLL 'KING' PRESLEY DIES

Across

1. Advance a theory in favour of sterling (8)
5. Undercover walk for Noah's helper, say (6)
8. In clubland it's handy for Paddy (10)
9. Is unable to betray hypocrisy (4)
10. Whereby surveyors kept Pa from Poppins country? (5-5, 4)
11. *Alter-ego*—only a new word for it (7)
13. Sort of swallow one cocktail (7)
15. Tribesmen flog a vehicle, we hear (7)
18. Senator sees trouble about ascetic sect (7)
21. Unsatisfactory end of Orpheus's date with Eurydice? (14)
22. Confound or partially ruin (4)
23. Adds signature to car sales charts? (10)
24. A willing suitor, Peggotty found him (6)
25. Offer beginning of lyric, with affection (8)

Down

1. Job on island for a card-carrier? (7)
2. Following errors they're often excepted (9)
3. Arden tree carver (7)
4. High-class students in tiny disturbance. A mere nothing (7)
5. Attic dwellers (9)
6. Gilbert's Lord Chancellor, crossing Salisbury Plain (7)
7. Like that infernal comedy-writer? (7)
12. Mountains wrongly presented in rag maps (9)
14. Sounds like a fashionable ring for Boniface (9)
16. Virgil's second thoughts? (7)
17. Barefooted supporter in church? Certainly not (7)
18. Record one volume in shortened form (7)
19. In stitches in the theatre, perhaps (7)
20. Content to make a statement about misfits (7)

25 JULY 1978

FIRST TEST TUBE BABY IS BORN,
A 5LB 12OZ GIRL

Across

1. Henceforth, we hope, like ever-rolling streams (5)
4. Unwilling to undertake role of bird-watcher (6-3)
9. Such shady dealing is not on the cards (9)
10. This tea contained in this teapot (5)
11. Are these sins so dull? (6)
12. Jesuit confounded giant with Scottish name (8)
14. Sporting facility for a hundred in resort (10)
16. Tobacco 100p? (4)
19. 6 disturbance describable as 'a —— of colour'? (4)
20. Horrified about engineer being so dressed (10)
22. Georgia only included in The Spirit of America (8)
23. A pig-stealer, I see—say, what energy! (6)
26. Point to resident magistrate in rage (5)
27. Meaning a worker of some consequence (9)
28. The law can ride on to destruction (9)
29. Chucked one into the outhouse (5)

Down

1. Big noise in 26 no longer silenced (9)
2. Aimed to disrupt means of communication (5)
3. £1 in copper in certain circumstances for clerical garb (8)
4. Over-grill this fish? (4)
5. First man up on a 22 *ac* vehicle in the island (10)
6. Like (Grand?) National characteristics? (6)
7. Some lords are betting on one form of ceremony (9)
8. Long story without point (5)
13. Capital punishment the 1 *ac* has survived (10)
15. Angry comment to its prolonged absence? (9)
17. Devoted many to one furry friend indeed (9)
18. The face including, in 1 *ac*, this 15 *dn* (8)
21. Roman priest who starts a Spanish dance (6)
22. Contributes to giving us total enjoyment (5)
24. I'm up and about after midnight in Florida (5)
25. Initially all public sessions end in recess (4)

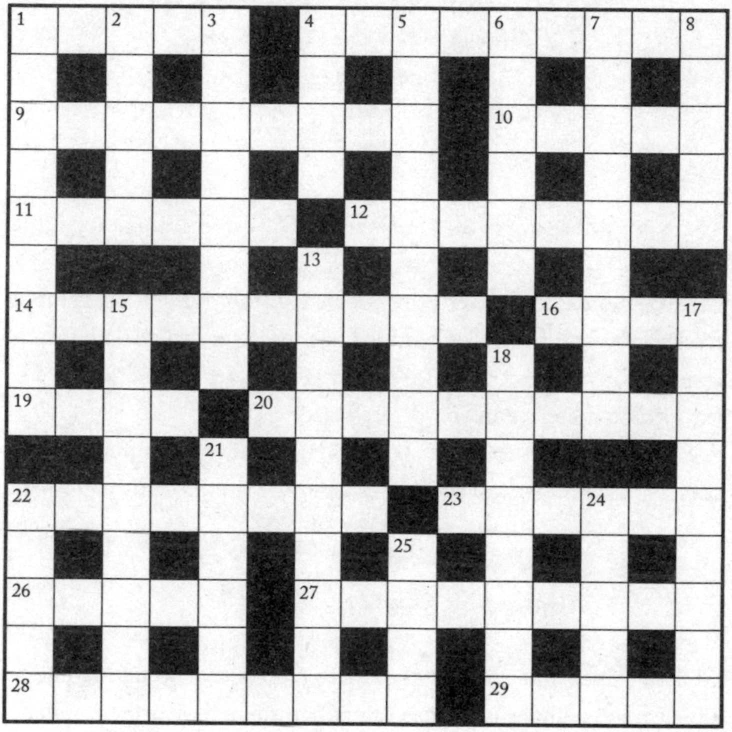

13 NOVEMBER 1979

TIMES RESUMES PUBLICATION AFTER YEAR-LONG SHUTDOWN

EXTRACTS FROM JOHN GRANT'S SCRAPBOOK

Editor of The Times Crossword, 1983–1995

There are three things that are vital to *The Times* – the letters, the obituaries and the crosswords. People get absolutely hooked on the crosswords. It's rather a sort of British thing, the most famous example of its kind in the world. There is always the desire in this country for the witty, urbane, almost gentle sort of diversion – for the gifted amateur, not the professional.

The solver must, above all, be entertained. It is not our aim to show how clever we are and provide puzzles that nobody can solve.

Gathering Round the Tribal Totem

The first thing one realizes about this club is that some member, somewhere, will always know more than the crossword compiler or editor. '*Revolutionary leader, such as William II*' (answer: REDHEAD) seemed harmless until a member pointed out that William's nickname Rufus derived from his ruddy complexion and not from the colour of his hair (as the *DNB* confirms).

Famous Solvers

Perhaps the greatest pleasure of my editorship was the relationship with our solvers, who were always polite and friendly. One such was Sir John Gielgud, who wrote to me a dozen years ago:

'It is true I am a crossword addict whose efforts were strenuously begun in 1944, when one of the electricians at the Haymarket staggered me with his crossword expertise. He could also follow a cue-sheet by the lines in a Shakespearean play without referring to numbers – after a long familiarity with seasons when he had worked at the Old Vic. Since that time I have found the crossword a sovereign therapy during endless hours of waiting while filming and doing television.'

Handing over the Mantle

But tomorrow's puzzle is by my successor as Editor of *The Times* Crossword, Brian Greer. I probably won't be able to solve it, because compilers are not generally good solvers, rather as composers of end-game problems sometimes do not even play chess. Indeed, I remember my predecessor Edmund Akenhead, at a *Times* Crossword Championship after his retirement, solving one of the puzzles in 23 minutes, which was widely acclaimed until it turned out to be one of his own.

A VISIT FROM MI5

The crossword in this book for the year 1966 was submitted by my father, Edmund Akenhead, and appeared in *The Times* two days before George Blake was sprung from Wormwood Scrubs. George Blake had served five years of a 42-year sentence for spying for Russia and, at that time, this was the longest term for such an offence ever imposed in a British court. Blake, who had served with distinction in the Dutch resistance against the Nazi regime during World War II and later with SOE, was not without his sympathizers. The authorities subsequently paid my father a visit, suspecting him of signalling the breakout with cryptic messages in *The Times* Crossword. They grilled him in his study for an entire morning, and I heard most of the interrogation. It is true that there are a number of uncomfortable coincidences in this crossword in clues and solutions alike which appear to signal not only the intention (12 *ac*, 4 *dn*, and 14 *dn*) but also the location (27 *ac*) and the means (11 *ac* and 1 *ac*); and with clues like 13 *ac* and with two references to the Scottish play (and ironically, George Blake did break a limb!) it is not surprising suspicions were aroused. My father was a magician who relished secrecy, yet on this occasion he was able to demonstrate that his puzzle had been submitted to the typesetters three weeks earlier, and he was absolved on these grounds. Yet, the whole incident remains a tantalizing mystery.

David Akenhead

THE EIGHTIES

Across

1. Viceroy—fellow who left things to others? (10)
9. Self-assertive pups I replaced by end of March (6)
10. Prevalent, the same classic content in heroic work (8)
11. Fish from Bala perhaps—the middle part (8)
12. A number of Frenchmen in a tribal division (4)
13. Undisguisedly fair, like the managing director? (5-5)
15. Main canvas used for drawing? (7)
17. A pound rate change in Canada (7)
20. Titania's boy 'so sweet a ——' (10)
21. Caesar's father not right in the head (4)
23. Where a young sucker hopes to get his lolly (4-4)
25. One not favoured by our betters (8)
26. Hills where we get magpies? (6)
27. Dumbfounded, having lost the address? (10)

Down

2. Enjoin one to get some piano pieces (6)
3. Old northern workers had a smashing time? (8)
4. Appoint about four, in this case (10)
5. Figure for month, past the quarter (7)
6. Stupefied and upset a foreign doctor (4)
7. A beef-brained glutton in Crete? (8)
8. Hackneyed article about unusually dear lawyers (10)
12. Professional beggars? (10)
14. Full of praise for clue I got—is different (10)
16. Looking for the key to the school (8)
18. Particular directions on cooking plaice (8)
19. Arrange that medicine swallowed is soft (7)
22. Buildings for break-down trucks (6)
24. His direction disconcerted the actor? (4)

2 JANUARY 1980

STEEL WORKERS STRIKE OVER PAY

Across

1. 'What a world of happiness their harmony foretells' (Poe) (7, 5)
9. Omar's 'Guest's Star- —— on the Grass'—like confetti? (9)
10. Ship's timbers from the principality (5)
11. The country happy in Latin style (6)
12. Force to accept money? How original! (8)
13. It's clear one gets married quietly in a hat (6)
15. Detail is arranged by one who seeks perfection (8)
18. Beaten by kind hearts (Tennyson) (8)
19. Church ceremonies appear wise between us (6)
21. What gives a so-called cardinal a good view? (8)
23. Free entry to French-style ball or marriage-feast (6)
26. Many a theatre cat following a star (5)
27. A call to battle by Conan Doyle's professor? (9)
28. Future king no coot, say the Cockneys (4, 8)

Down

1. Festive occasion was put on canvas (7)
2. Lady with whom Burlington Bertie had a banana (5)
3. No reason for such knowledge in teaching (9)
4. Dress for a queen in much of the UK (4)
5. Source of gold a doodler maybe dreamed of (8)
6. Many sheep in Sussex (5)
7. Nanny's first in pigtail-making (8)
8. A trail followed—to the throne? (6)
14. The Bard's true minds thereby united (8)
16. Country accepts a pupil, as this did a royal one (9)
17. Used for racing—not rounding up cattle (5-3)
18. Like the icy contents of 18 *ac*, losing nothing (6)
20. Foreigner is in a way outstanding (7)
22. Directions a girl has to follow (5)
24. Young Lochinvar came 'to —— at our 23' and ran off with Ellen (5)
25. Mute witness of Tara's 12 glory (4)

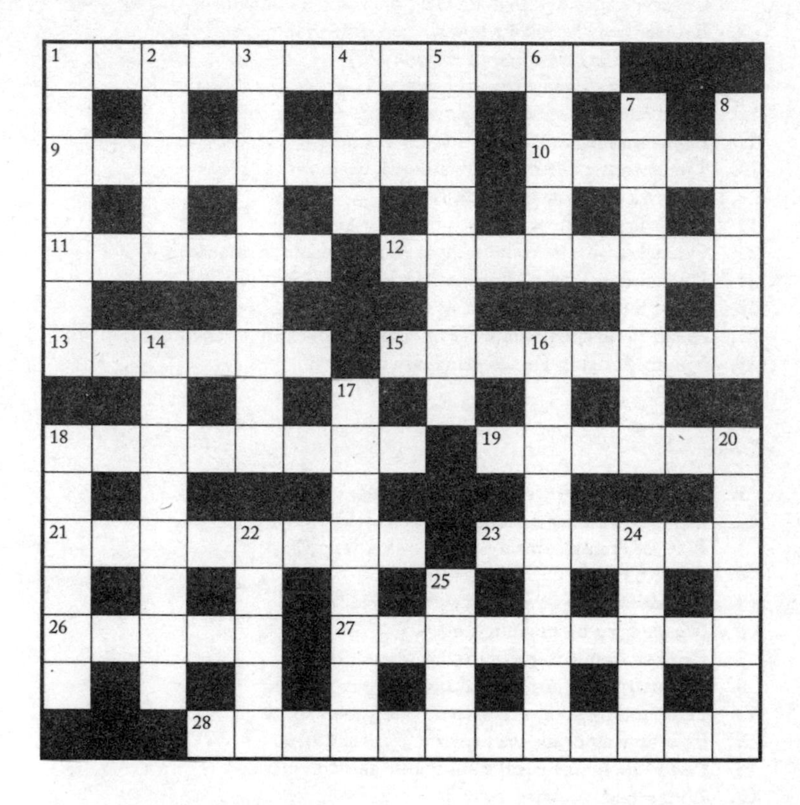

29 JULY 1981

CHARLES AND DIANA MARRY

Across

1. Cheer imitated at Harfleur (5)
4. Recover from knockout blow in corner (4, 5)
9. No squash in this scene of action (4, 5)
10. Features of straightforward leaders (5)
11. Mind out—a society can provide such amusement (9, 6)
12. Boy inserts parts of ad in this, for example (6)
14. Timepiece unable to strike one? (8)
17. It proves unusually playful (8)
19. Lord's house (6)
22. One takes interest in helping to accommodate members (8, 7)
24. It's found in Texas, Alabama and Missouri (5)
25. Water for a mother pig (5, 4)
26. Make disclosure on number of deliveries—extra population (9)
27. Minor official in French bank, say (5)

Down

1. In which rash Scots may go astray (9)
2. Broke down after midnight in Wales (5)
3. Roe, for example, from one fish? In a way (7)
4. Relative's money split by us (6)
5. Jack supporting Christian, for example (8)
6. Writer did a bit of smuggling (7)
7. Remove from cover in sun's heat here (9)
8. Attractive little girl has a fling (5)
13. Hate putting a lot of money in crew, so to speak (9)
15. Free-flowing drink, we hear, on Thames (9)
16. Performer he managed sang with evil manipulation (8)
18. Boring outside broadcast (7)
20. Zola was one such in charge (7)
21. Country is overthrowing unfortunate monarch (6)
22. Said to applaud a hired ruffian (5)
23. Best type? That's the size of it (5)

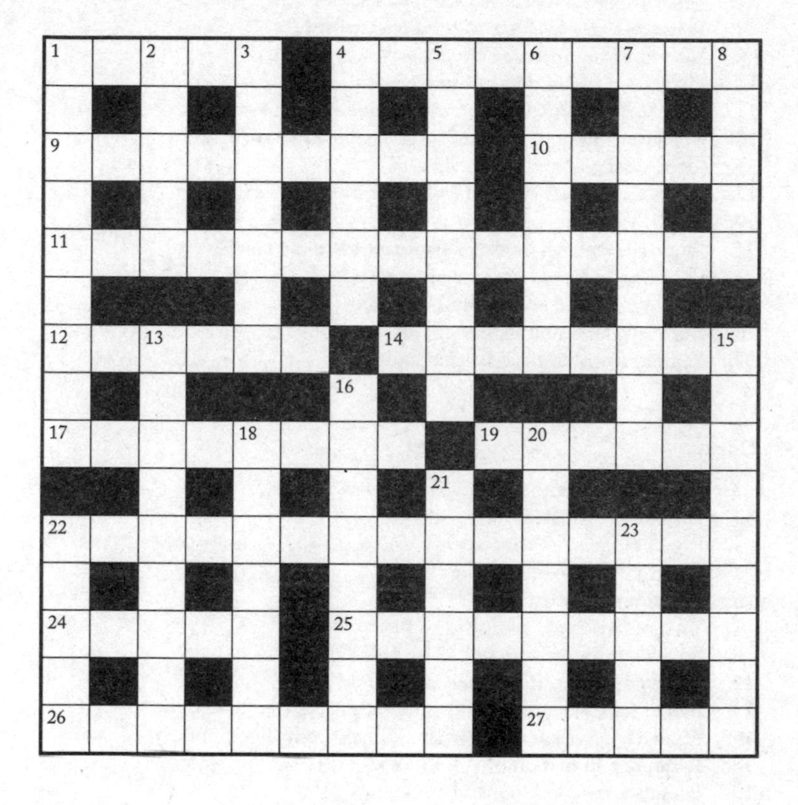

29 MAY 1982

POPE MAKES HISTORIC VISIT TO CANTERBURY

Across

1. You can't go through the card if you stick to these courses (5, 5)
9. A suitable case for referring to the Receiver (6)
10. Like sops well stirred—the nursery sort perhaps (3-5)
11. Helps you change, but not into clerical gear (3-5)
12. Knocked back in cricket practice, this shooter (4)
13. Scholar of Merton, obviously a man of letters (10)
15. Don't do it—it's a burden (7)
17. Write on the back the place of which we hear directions? (7)
20. Maybe steep parts of these to check, e.g., acidity (4, 6)
21. Betrayed, especially when down river (4)
23. Resolute chap to drag army of women back (8)
25. This sums up those who multiply quickly (8)
26. Been lacerated a bit by corset? (6)
27. Conservative Bar head has ingenuity (10)

Down

2. One may be seen hanging around a low joint (6)
3. Periodical heed-taker (8)
4. Fly from Polish road accident (10)
5. Order new-style silk for memorial (7)
6. Whirl round Mary Baker (4)
7. The less welcome of Kipling's impostors (8)
8. So address 13 on stationery ? (6-4)
12. Crooked shyster, apt to make Scots hop (10)
14. Italian (of course) thick but full of beans (10)
16. Strangely prescient about what L drivers may do on holiday (8)
18. Is Bondi a formation of volcanic rock? (8)
19. Sounds a suitable bird on the menu (4-3)
22. Some crumpet, often toasted (6)
24. Smart lad wanted (4)

17 JANUARY 1983

BBC WAKES UP TO MORNING TV

Across

1. Fairies manage to provide optical assistance (9)
6. No time to damage footwear (5)
9. Avenger is after retreating Londoners, perhaps (7)
10. Racing about with a gun, lots of soldiers (7)
11. The turning-point of the match, in general (5)
12. Man in the back with girl, getting practice (9)
13. With some relief, managed to follow me back (8)
15. Hold the fort (4)
19. Sharp, a note within the range (4)
20. Think about arranging time and date (8)
23. Mercenary general, retired into the country (4-5)
24. Being subject to error (5)
26. Against what, to the French, is dated (7)
27. Compact, non-profit-making organization does (7)
28. Dog that's a Nobel prize-winner (5)
29. Fail to take advantage of a war. Why? To order! (5, 4)

Down

1. Counterfeit coin under control; note held (9)
2. Italic type? Yes and no (5)
3. Susan keeping Sir Patrick in uncertainty (8)
4. One who watches over irregular verbs within (8)
5. Your attention given first to what is unrefined (6)
6. Communication of note (6)
7. Miss Everdene married David (9)
8. Dog-end—that's about right (5)
14. Guard one starting game, accepting pay rise (9)
16. Initially passionate meeting of boy and girl could result in it (9)
17. Winter days frozen up, without one bit of fire (8)
18. Scratch, having a tie (8)
21. Exclusive group in a club, we hear (6)
22. Divide tinned order (6)
23. Money for composer without a royalty (5)
25. End up with a cry of pain, a beastly cry (5)

14 FEBRUARY 1984

OLYMPIC GOLD FOR TORVILL AND DEAN

Across

1. Lord of the Rings supplanted by Jove! (6)
4. This analysis used by physicists rather than by ghost-hunters (8)
10. Effect of fire on skin—note by surgeon (7)
11. It's right to pass by this work by Vanbrugh (7)
12. Drinking—your pardon humbly craved (10)
13. Tendency, in a wood, to go off course (4)
15. Wooden O as scene of Henry V's operations (7)
17. Lift-off for a social climber? (7)
19. Aggressive and bombastic speech about a member (7)
21. Line that's usually hot (7)
23. Secret society (singularly unsuited for getting coal) (4)
24. Like Jowett of Balliol, involved in Economist, nothing less (10)
27. Sign for Spanish camping accommodation (7)
28. Like a paramount chief's working wear (7)
29. Bit of guts first shown by one in empire outpost (8)
30. Manx pawnbroker, notice, with nothing on (6)

Down

1. Boss tries to reform writer of tear-jerkers (3-6)
2. Involve little Tom and opposite number in idle revolution (7)
3. Disconcert some, turning up in a heap (6-4)
5. True, a chap in trouble needs it to join the Caterpillar Club (9)
6. A swindle, say, may land you here in prison (4)
7. Copy material, £1 about (7)
8. City's in front, we hear (5)
9. Actor in Arden for instance (4)
14. Nice touches spoiled when one's gone and blotted it (10)
16. Financial forecasts include one million in landed property (9)
18. Controlled engine speed, but told her otherwise about the race (9)
20. Lowest of the three kingdoms (7)
22. Part of a girl in work that's extremely hard (3-4)
23. Putting a spinner in charge is what they talk about (5)
25. What an adorable figure! (4)
26. Near the average (4)

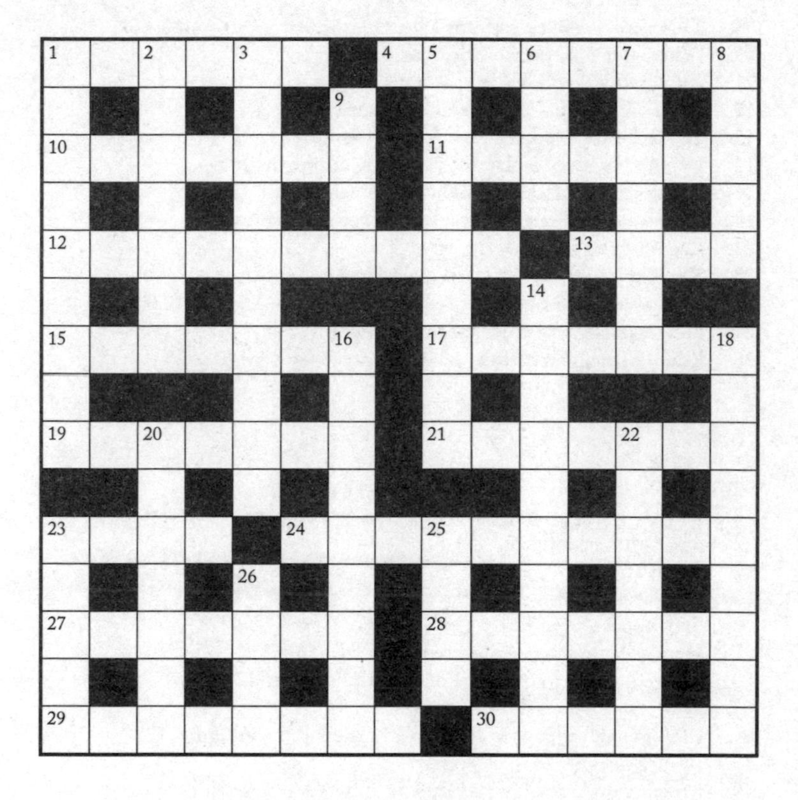

13 JULY 1985

LIVE AID MAKES MILLIONS FOR AFRICA

Across

1. Summarize yield again (12)
8. This cake is cooked for fans (7)
9. Where one may be sent for carrying a gun! (7)
11. An island girl cuddles in this way (7)
12. Medical problem dramatized by GBS? (7)
13. Too fat to be in pearly queen's stockings (5)
14. Naboth's produce stolen for scattering on the field (5-4)
16. Fail to respond to alarm about huntsman's return (9)
19. Bishop introduces everyone separately at the seaside (5)
21. Beginning to subscribe shortly (7)
23. Shady profiteers decapitated by low beams (7)
24. It follows advance publicity (7)
25. Old sectarian was 'arder up than a widow (7)
26. Yell, possibly, to get small glass for little beast (8, 4)

Down

1. Ascribe extremes of eloquence to this judge (7)
2. Anxiety about attempt to secure the compound (7)
3. Star writer's confusion? (9)
4. Some of the worst epidemics happen where it's warmish (5)
5. Fish swallows sick girl (7)
6. Signal success put him right out (7)
7. He should be interested in what you have in mind (12)
10. Allow old king to conceal box near Cambridge (12)
15. Printer's sign an MP reads out (9)
17. Monumental tribute to Herbert by Oriental theatre-goers (7)
18. Ability, it's said, to make a pan (7)
19. Member of Antediluvian Order in New York State? (7)
20. Pleasing feature? See me in any case about it (7)
22. Some grub for the French girl on the banks of the river (5)

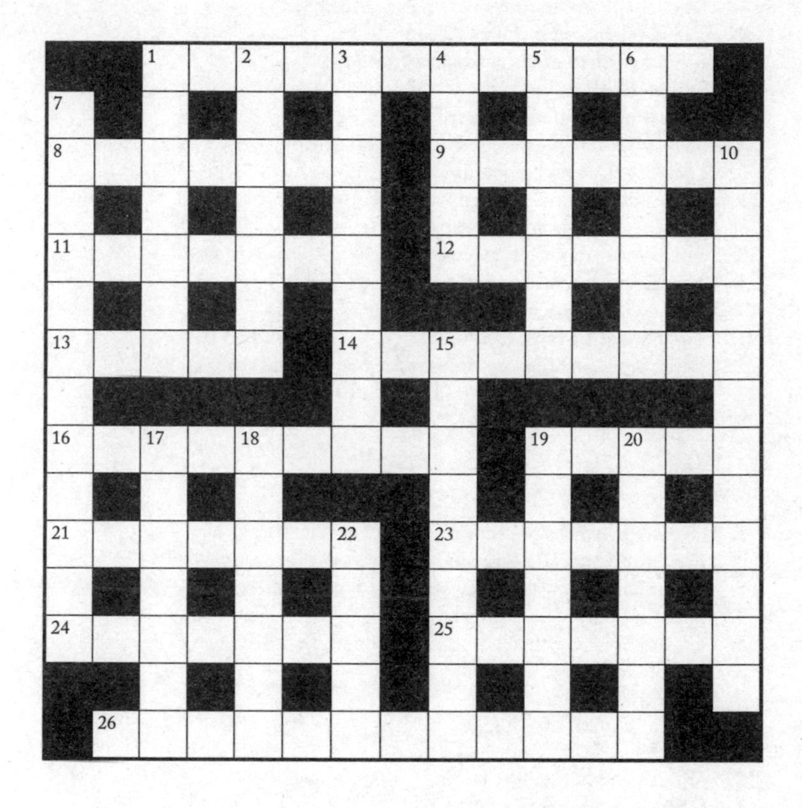

27 JANUARY 1986

SEVEN DEAD IN SPACE SHUTTLE CHALLENGER DISASTER

Across

1. Rush about with bottle-opener and drink (5)
4. Keeps going for brochures (9)
9. A fighting man holds with juicy fruit (9)
10. Studies English, being stupid (5)
11. Actress ignoring bill for hair (5)
12. He'll have designs on any who patronise him (9)
13. 19 *dn* could be such a manipulator! (7)
15. A ship the lawmen go ahead and occupy (7)
18. Frank seeing that soldiers join up (7)
20. Broadcast parts of TT races (7)
21. Neat figure—with the hips under restraint! (9)
23. Approach a junction. There's a long tailback (5)
25. Light-weight animal (5)
26. Demonstration about courts that lack a dominant woman (9)
27. A speculator sees the upswing in gold (9)
28. A king, and so majestic (5)

Down

1. Occasionally moulds seem moist (9)
2. Row involving cattle-grazing (5)
3. The money that's about may be used for underwear (9)
4. His work output is impressive! (7)
5. Go too high and there's nothing green and nothing soft (7)
6. Its speakers arrive by air (5)
7. Temperate land mass (9)
8. Caught a whiff of fish (5)
14. Nice teens fashion awareness (9)
16. Directions on bridging, leaving no loopholes (9)
17. Withdrew, a little hurt (9)
19. A scholar, given time, adds up (7)
20. 'Pains of love be —— far than all other pleasures are.' (Dryden) (7)
21. Portly porter (5)
22. Control the beast! (5)
24. A girl will take many a look back (5)

1		2		3	■	4		5		6		7		8
	■		■		■		■		■		■		■	
9									■	10				
	■		■		■		■		■		■		■	
11					■	12								
	■	■	■		■		■		■	■	■		■	■
13		14					■	15		16				17
	■		■		■	■	■	■	■		■		■	
18						19	■	20						
■	■		■	■	■		■		■		■	■	■	
21				22					■	23		24		
	■		■		■		■		■		■		■	
25					■	26								
	■		■		■		■		■		■		■	
27									■	28				

19 OCTOBER 1987

BLACK MONDAY
STOCK MARKET CRISIS

Across

1. Do hardy men relax, having achieved their objective? (4,3,3)
9. Dan Cupid? (6)
10. To get fish, man takes to a boat (4,4)
11. Beetle—boy written about by one Rudyard, heartlessly (8)
12. Issue a note to produce this (4)
13. Poem about a beautiful woman, a queen (7,3)
15. Polish poet I put in hospital (7)
17. Part of Russia is taken aback by chief of police (7)
20. Individual I have to pay proper attention to at first (10)
21. Every time a chap's taken in (4)
23. Overwhelm one woman in order to get an appointment (8)
25. Irregular policemen about to cover up disastrous raid (8)
26. Does get confused about copper coin (6)
27. Prime Minister with duller brain (4,6)

Down

2. No oxygen left inside the city (6)
3. Be in one wagon—topless, but it's got nine sides (8)
4. Doubtful accession involving left of revivalist movement (10)
5. Any gold can be transmuted in twenty-four hours (7)
6. Carrier brought up in court here (4)
7. How did water get into the river? It's a mystery (8)
8. 14's way, by sound of it (6,4)
12. One who looks solemn and then moreover, runs inside (10)
14. Benedick, a new union member (10)
16. Engineer beginning to show ingenuity (8)
18. Jumbo, the plane that's been redesigned (8)
19. Craft rising city provided (7)
22. It takes one aboard a vessel (6)
24. Eager to work in silver (4)

3 DECEMBER 1988

EGG INDUSTRY FURY OVER SALMONELLA CLAIM

Across

1. Heavy material left in Welsh lake by Soviet extremists (7)
5. A speed reached by soldiers with a Greek vessel (7)
9. Gaseous element a man discovered around Gateshead (5)
10. Grasping parent in car, returning with evidence of debts (9)
11. Weapon for a domineering woman (9)
12. Main element in viva voce, an inquisition (5)
13. Woman removes head of chapel (5)
15. Books of a woman sage written in a different way (9)
18. Champion is terrific when drinking wine! (9)
19. Half-heartedly cleaned up the bike (5)
21. Huge bird eating a hard fish (5)
23. It can serve as tinder, barring ill luck! (9)
25. Temporary quarters by river, sited around a bell-tower (9)
26. Possibly active part for musicians? (5)
27. A group broke bread, some say, after a month (7)
28. Head off jogger in New York from the convent (7)

Down

1. Shrub found by bishop on leisurely stroll (7)
2. On the rocks? Not with this floating asset (9)
3. Declare invalid, removing article from book (5)
4. Discharge sailor displaying change of attitude (9)
5. Drink swallowed very quietly—a temptation once! (5)
6. This represents a word for a North Briton with no pulse (9)
7. Bracing air an individual associated with a wizard place (5)
8. How like a winter Shakespeare's had been (7)
14. Tragic Latin hero—one of exceptional courage (4-5)
16. Such a labour, making her char around University (9)
17. When one's caught inside, better to ad-lib (9)
18. Wind thus restricting heads of relief organization on business (7)
20. Decrepit stranger in the borders of Dahomey (7)
22. Accept a foreign currency—it is underwritten (5)
23. Theist's first observance, worn out by constant repetition (5)
24. Holy books found in bird sanctuary (5)

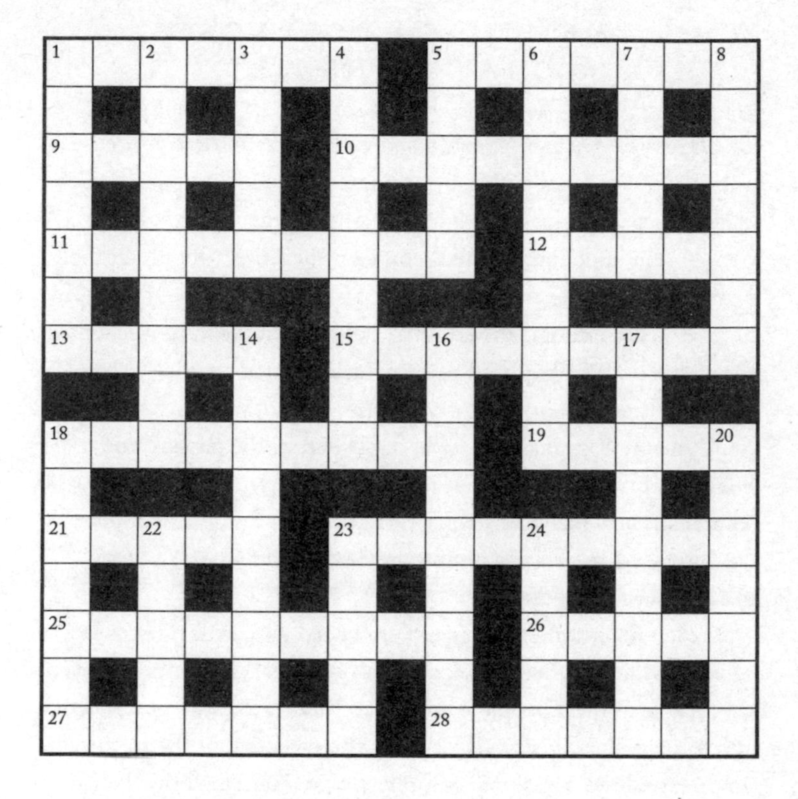

9 NOVEMBER 1989

BERLIN WALL COMES DOWN

THE TIMES CROSSWORD CHAMPIONSHIP

The Crossword Championship started in 1970 and ran regularly until 2000. Potential entrants completed a qualifying puzzle published in the paper at the beginning of the year, which was of the normal standard; and a correct entry entitled them to attend the regional final of their choice – there were generally six of these, in hotels in cities around the country, held over a series of weekends through the summer. London, even with two finals, always had more applicants than could be accommodated, so they had to face the fearsome Eliminator puzzle, published in the paper during February and so difficult that normally even entries that had several answers blank or wrong still qualified. Some Londoners used to avoid the Eliminator altogether by applying to other centres, even Glasgow.

At each final, contestants were presented with four puzzles to solve, with half an hour for each. Many contestants simply enjoyed the chance to meet people who shared their interest in crosswords, and to meet the Crossword Editor (who attended in the role of umpire) and the occasional compilers who dared to show their faces; but for serious competitors it was a race against the clock: bonus points were awarded, one for each minute under thirty that a puzzle was finished, and there were always a good number of people with all-correct solutions, so that the winners were invariably decided on bonus points. Each minute as it passed was marked off on a slide projected on the wall, and a well-drilled team from a local school patrolled the aisles, responding to a competitor's raised hand clutching the completed puzzle by hastening to their place to collect the entry and mark the time on to it. Behind the scenes, another team worked accurately at great speed to mark the answers and transfer the scores to a results grid.

A tea interval was taken after the third puzzle; the results to date were then posted on the walls, so that everyone could see how they were doing, and the front runners knew how much time they could afford over the final puzzle. The last puzzle was marked equally speedily and the winners were announced as soon as the final thirty minutes were up. Generally, three or four qualifiers were allowed from each of the regional finals, so that the national final had around two dozen contestants, including usually the reigning champion who was given a bye to the following year's final.

In 1995, the winner was Dr Helen Ougham, a scientist from Wales. Helen started solving crosswords in her teens, and was soon enjoying both *The Times* and harder crosswords, such as the *Listener*. She entered the competition first as an undergraduate, just for the fun of it and to meet other solvers; but then life and work took over, and she did not return to the competition for some years. She won the Birmingham final in 1989, and qualified for the national final again in 1991, in which she came fifth. But she approached the Birmingham competition in 1995 with no particular expectation, and remembers little of it, except that she found the puzzle the present editor compiled gratifyingly easy! She finished in third place, which qualified her once more for the national final, along with a stiff field of 21 containing five other previous champions and twelve other previous national finalists.

So to the Hyatt Carlton Hotel in Cadogan Place on Saturday 30 September for the final. Helen recalls: 'My newly acquired partner and I had to leave home at a quarter to five for the train journey to

London. My mother also came up, from Kent, and this was their first meeting. I think it was more stressful for them than for me; by the end of the last puzzle, they had their arms around each other, eyes shut, and couldn't bear to wait for the result! I knew as I finished the fourth puzzle that I must be somewhere in contention, but it wasn't until the organizer Mike Rich came up and whispered that he thought I had a good chance of winning that I started to think about the short speech I might have to make if I did. I must have said something, although it all passed in a blur.'

It was a tight finish: although Helen solved the four, difficult puzzles in an average of 11 minutes each – one of them in just six – in a nerve-racking finale she beat Michael Macdonald-Cooper (a previous champion, and later to be the crossword editor of *The Independent*) by a mere half a minute, with the defending champion William Pilkington (chief budget officer of the then Cleveland County Council) just a further half-minute behind.

Helen says: 'That year there was no sponsor, so I didn't win a gallon of whisky or a year's first-class rail travel; but I received a beautiful glass punch-bowl, which is still on my mantelpiece, and I was glad my partner was there to help carry it back on the train to Aberystwyth!'

Did winning make a difference to her life? 'Not in the least. I went back to work, which started to involve me in a certain amount of travel. Although these pressures meant I could not always take part in the final, I returned in 1996 to defend my title, though with conspicuous lack of success that time. I did get asked to go on *Countdown*, though – but I never did.'

Richard Browne

THE 1995 COMPETITION

Across

1. Such an affair, if it got about, could become exceptionally bellicose (12)
9. Quality of the loud-speaker in the foyer (9)
10. Character-building in the Army (5)
11. The art, when concealed, of the tile-maker (6)
12. Cloggy sort of pudding excites Jack's wit (8)
13. Powerful sort of service from one not quite a gentleman (6)
15. Poet cut by Oriental medico (8)
18. Born nurse comprehends the lung (8)
19. Fleshy animal (6)
21. Source of screech owl's cry on high branch (8)
23. Moving quickly, cast set about 'The Last of Mrs Cheyney' (6)
26. The Red Queen took precedence, but slipped up (5)
27. Funny cartoon about the lieutenant's low woman (9)
28. The coaches are going round the reservoir (7-5)

Down

1. Apprentice wearing coarse material (7)
2. Pet standing up—it wants to be understood (5)
3. Fruit turnover readily available from this carrier (5-4)
4. Very dry individual in a way (4)
5. The key to starting revolutions (8)
6. A non-drinker in charge in a high position (5)
7. Jacobson in a predicament in African republic (8)
8. Did he notice the finches in Australia? (6)
14. Start shooting 'The Gaping Inferno' (4, 4)
16. They are often fired, which may be why we are short-handed (5, 4)
17. Brave Napoleonic music espoused by the hard left (8)
18. Little Boy Blue, for example, and the black cow (6)
20. Running, say, on side to be effective (7)
22. Hotel, unfinished monster, came to nothing (5)
24. Soldier set up card game in blockhouse (5)
25. Characterless girl is out of love (4)

This puzzle was solved within 30 minutes by 95% of the contestants.

1 2 3 4 5 6 7 8 9 10 11 12 13 14 15 16 17 18 19 20 21 22 23 24 25 26 27 28

1995 NATIONAL FINAL

PUZZLE NO. 1

Across

1. Powerful leader one should read carefully (8)
5. Work in college (6)
10. Walk *East* to America? Certain to be a tragedy (10, 5)
11. Politician doing well to make himself agreeable (7)
12. The class is detailed to move bookcase (7)
13. It was simple to be Roman emperor (8)
15. French publication largely a failure (5)
18. Examination of half the theatre (5)
20. Very angry, recognize problem (8)
23. Spiked attachment, the key to operating on a slope (7)
25. Stopped ball in deviation of flight (7)
26. Comment by judge is a small blow (7, 8)
27. A quarter got the hidden error (6)
28. Wide boy may at last appear in court (8)

Down

1. Reproduce notes, having chosen to speak (6)
2. Middle of the road—the ground of real value to government (5, 4)
3. Different name given to the same flower (7)
4. Go over actor's script (5)
6. It's said to include part of circuit (7)
7. Luxurious extra hour (5)
8. Border pine in covert (8)
9. Is being in the shade a bore? (8)
14. Loss of marbles for Elgin at last—is it any surprise? (8)
16. Chap with title needs to knock about (9)
17. *Guardian* to be alert to trick by KGB centre (8)
19. One up the pole—health broken by news from radio (7)
21. Marx, working, used to attack Leviathan (7)
22. The White King? (6)
24. Passage through middle of Scottish town (5)
25. Youthful novel (5)

This puzzle was solved within 30 minutes by 81% of the contestants.

1 2 3 4 5 6 7 8
9
10
11 12
13 14 15 16
17
18 19 20 21
22
23 24 25
26
27 28

1995 NATIONAL FINAL

PUZZLE NO. 2

Across

1. A bit of a bore with money for wine (10)
6. Lead of whom a member must follow? (4)
9. Piece of harness that'll make better profit sooner or later (10)
10. Garment is wrapped around artist's back (4)
12. To sell drugs illegally is offensive (4)
13. Might it contain tot's head, and hair also? (6,3)
15. Exposed liberal to public (4,4)
16. Tree damaged, caught by wings of powerful bird (6)
18. Heart led by opponents at bridge—play another! (6)
20. Within a short time, investment appears ill-judged (8)
23. No leniency here—for those involved with rackets? (4,5)
24. Provide information linking gang-leader to offence (4)
26. It's a very old wicket, so declare (4)
27. Cold drink container English fan wanted after victory (4-6)
28. City, after half-time, barely extended (4)
29. His father was a detective (10)

Down

1. Firm doctor appears to get shock under control (4)
2. Silver ring on sea-bed (7)
3. Book that's witty about pop music (8,4)
4. Record organ part (8)
5. Home established and superficially decorated (6)
7. Moorish cover girl (7)
8. Blunt nib and paper without writing (5-5)
11. Favour including as weight valuable piece of basalt (7,5)
14. Valentine card given after piece of music's heard (10)
17. Teacher putting mark one point up (8)
19. Box around ring, only to be laid out on canvas later? (7)
21. Small ruler used in making letters (7)
22. Champ taken round one European city (6)
25. Goose put in inferior oven without any stuffing (4)

This puzzle was solved within 30 minutes by 86% of the contestants.

1995 NATIONAL FINAL

PUZZLE NO. 3

Across

1. Change into suit (6)
4. I am permitted to accept money, that's understood (8)
10. Impressed by a number of points in connection with the business (9)
11. In a quite normal voice (5)
12. A quid a month brought in by Indian (7)
13. Many men put out about end.of affaire (7)
14. Taken in school—oral (5)
15. Stretch in solitary for concealing gun after completion of crime (8)
18. Gold from the mint (5-3)
20. Speaking of Christmas, I'll provide for the next generation (5)
23. USA gold rebuilt island capital (7)
25. Pitman's books about deity (7)
26. In the autumn London yuppy heads for the country (5)
27. It helps in shooting deer—a lot (9)
28. Other people catch trains, in the main (3,5)
29. Sails finally subside to deck (6)

Down

1. Bishop smuggled guerrilla's arms (8)
2. In Manila, leading man jumps into bed (7)
3. Principal bottles up rebuke to a pupil appearing early (9)
5. Doting mum keeps on, and I reach a decision (4,2,4,4)
6. Stop rent increase (3-2)
7. A note; formerly, it was a crotchet (7)
8. Where kings are seated and unseated, by the sound of it (6)
9. Abandoned wife—send her eau de Cologne—a valediction (3,11)
16. Composite set comprises several games (9)
17. Pear-tree could make a come-back (8)
19. Keen, outstanding person turned up and dined (7)
21. Honourable and noted music-maker (7)
22. A bank out of touch (6)
24. Better counsel wife to leave (5)

This puzzle was solved within 30 minutes by 95% of the contestants.

1995 NATIONAL FINAL

PUZZLE NO. 4

PUBLIC REACTIONS TO THE CROSSWORD CHAMPIONSHIP

Crossword SOS

Sir, — My psychiatrist agrees that if you occasionally fibbed to note that, say, '99 per cent of the competitors at the Bristol/London/Edinburgh regional finals of *The Times* Knockando Crossword Championship took all day to solve just several of the above 30-odd clues', it would benefit me greatly.

Mr W. Sanderson

Puzzling it out

Sir, —Once again I note that a considerable proportion of contestants solved one of your crossword puzzles within 30 minutes. May I say that I should be most disappointed if anything like this happened to me.

Surrounded by dictionary, thesaurus and numerous reference books, my average is about two hours, during which despair is one of the usual phases, and sometimes I don't even finish, though it is surprising how the solving rate improves once the television has been turned off.

Mr R. M. Ward

Sir, —I was horrified to read that Mr Ward uses dictionaries et al in solving the crossword, since I was brought up to believe that 'looking up' was at best an admission of defeat and, at worst, downright cheating.

Surely the whole purpose of education is to enable one to complete *The Times* Crossword unaided?

Mr David Vince

Sir, —Surely Mr D. Vince has got it wrong? It is precisely the research into 'dictionaries et al' which furthers education and gives purpose to the completion of *The Times* Crossword.

Mr John Bloch

Sir, —I will give up reference books when I can be assured that the compiler has not used them.

Mr J. G. Edwards

Sir, —Well done the 51 per cent of competitors who completed the Manchester Regional Final of *The Times* Aberlour Crossword Championship within 30 minutes. In my home the crossword was completed by 100 per cent of the entrants in six hours. I was the sole entrant.

Please confirm that the same conditions applied for the finalists as myself: two impromptu breaks to converse with double-glazing salesmen; brief discussion with Jehovah's Witnesses; exchange of pleasantries (and cash) with a charity collector; break to prepare and cook dinner; chauffeur duties for children to various venues;

and momentary panic when I thought the ding dong of the bell meant it was all over but no, it was a lady selling cosmetics. Given these circumstances, didn't we do well!

Mrs G. M. Watt

Sir, — In the summer of 1999, I went to London to compete in the final of *The Times* Crossword Competition. I had little expectation of success, and lived up to that expectation by failing to complete any of the four puzzles in the allotted time.

After the final, I bumped into an acquaintance of mine from work, John Grimshaw – I am a Royal Air Force officer and John works for the Ministry of Defence. John is a regular compiler of *The Times* and *The Listener* crosswords, and he, together with the late Mike Rich, was organizing the event. I had nothing particular planned for the afternoon and I thought it would be interesting to stay, in any case, to watch the grand final, so I offered to help with setting up. John duly accepted, so I spent a couple of hours moving chairs and tables around and shuffling pieces of paper.

I thought little more about my minor role in that year's *Times* Crossword Competition, until a couple of months later I received a phone call from John. He suggested that I would be very interested in the following Saturday's crossword. Intrigued, I rushed out on Saturday to buy my copy of *The Times*. As I solved the clues, I was surprised and delighted to discover a hidden message. Four of the answers in order gave: SQUADRON LEADER, PETER, FLIPPANT, and THANKS.

Peter Flippant, Wing Commander

NEW CLUES FOR OLD

One way of looking at the world, personified by Kingsley Amis, is that every day, in every way, things are getting worse and worse. This is even less true than its converse, associated with Emile Coué, that every day, in every way, things are getting better and better. If challenged by a pessimist for an example of something that has improved during our lifetimes, offer him *The Times* Crossword.

Those primitive crosswords of 60 years ago were not entirely '*Anagram, 7 letters*' plain-sailing. The first one included clues that are early cryptics: '*A month, nothing more, in Ireland (4)*' – answer, 'MAY-O'. But for cryptographic cunning, elegance, and wit, today's crosswords are to yesteryear's as Hyperion to a satyr.

You could call one type of clue that has come in recently the Chimera clue, with a lion's head, an allusion's tail, and an anagram's body: that is, a clue that is part anagram and part something else. For example: '*Writ from man Maud's twisted (7)*' means Man + twist (i.e. an anagram of) Maud's = Mandamus (a writ from a superior court). The other new type of clue is the '& lit', that is to say an anagram + a literal description of the solution in the words of the anagram. This is the crème de la crème. For example: '*One red man possible (7)*' = an anagram of I (Roman numeral) red man = AMERIND. '*Involved* [anagram hint] *in my trio, one is this (8)*' = an anagram of '*in my trio*' = MINORITY.

Crosswords are amateur cryptographers, code-breakers – and spies. As it was said in the anxious months leading to D-Day an alarming number of code names used for the Normandy landings, such as Omaha and Utah, cropped up in crossword solutions. Paranoid puzzlers in the War Office suspected there was a Nazi spy lurking in the basement of Printing House Square sending cryptic messages to Berlin.

Over the years the lex of *The Times* Crossword has become more unbuttoned and informal, as has the language in other less specialized registers. Every day you find slang, racy words and double entendres that would not have been passed even 10 years ago. For example Bimbo, Bananas or Bats signifying (hint hint) Mad.

However, much of the idiolect of the setters of *The Times* Crosswords remains charmingly old-fashioned. A moll and a good-looker are quaint old male chauvinist gent's clues that point us towards a woman. The books that we are supposed to have read are still the reading-list of a Thirties English public school: the Bible (Authorized Version, natch) and Prayer Book, Shakespeare (particularly *Hamlet*), Dickens, Lewis Carroll (especially the three little girls in the well), Gilbert and Sullivan. As the times move on, we are expected to have read Evelyn Waugh (with particular reference to *Scoop*) and there has even been a clue from James Joyce, though this enraged some punters.

Philip Howard, 1990

CROSSWORDS:
ON A POINTLESS RITUAL

I am almost sure I am not from this planet.

It would be no surprise now if a great hand were to come down from the sky and scoop me up from where I stand (at the Underground station, staring at the escalator that has been broken for weeks yet nobody is fixing) and a great voice were to say 'Okay, Matthew, your testing time is over. You were right. They are all mad. But you are not one of them. You never were. Come and have a cup of tea and we'll explain the whole thing.' And I would be led away. I have been expecting this since I was a toddler. And the first thing I would want to ask is about crosswords.

In our pages opposite there has been a protracted correspondence going on, again, about these stupid things. I have never done a crossword in my life and I hope to die in the same condition. Why in heaven's name one man should want to spend his time guessing which letters 'go' in the little boxes devised by another man beats me. If they have so much spare time and need an intellectual challenge, why don't they learn how escalators work, then tell London Regional Transport?

Riddles, games and rituals. Yuk! I suppose *The Times* Crossword is really a triumphant and classy amalgam of all three. It is, they say, a sort of mental exercise. The intellectual equivalent of a caged hamster's exercise wheel.

But my friends, the cage door is open!

Matthew Parris, 1990

THE GREATEST SOLVER: JOHN SYKES

1929–1993

I was saddened to read the news of John Sykes' death in *The Times* last week. Like many of you, I had the greatest admiration for his linguistic prowess and speed of thought, which led him to ten victories in these annual championships.

At times we amateurs might have grumbled about having to pit our puny wits against a professional lexicographer – and there was no doubt that what he himself called a 'marginal advantage' put him head and shoulders above the rest of us.

I am reminded of the description of Julius Caesar that Shakespeare almost wrote:

Why man, he doth bestride the chequered grid
Like a colossus, and we petty men
Wilt under his huge brain, and peep about
To find ourselves perpetual runners-up.

I'm sure that we fellow competitors approached the finals with some trepidation. You might even say, in modern parlance, that we were 'Syked out'. At the top of his form John was unstoppable. In 1974 he completed the four puzzles in 29 minutes with a record margin of 12 minutes over his nearest rival. This means that he would have solved five puzzles in the time it took us to do four.

Unlike mine, his mental powers did not seem to deteriorate with age. In the 1989 final he averaged 7 minutes per puzzle, and at his last appearance in 1990 his average time was eight minutes. It was a tragedy that ill health prevented him from continuing.

John was essentially a *Times* Crossword man. He didn't care for the *Listener* or Azed puzzles, which he found 'too convoluted'. But strangely enough he wasn't a *Times* reader. So how did he perfect his expertise on the crossword? Well, it was reported that a friend used to give him a weekly batch of puzzles, and that he sat down and solved them all at once. He had hit the ideal training for these exacting competitions.

Roy Dean, 1993

Doctor Who Puts One Across (4, 5)

His technique was to start at 1 Across and then go to 1 Down, proceeding to the clues for which he had an initial letter wherever possible. One of his tricks was to give priority to solving the Down clues. 'I believe that setters usually start with the Across clues. They put some of their best subtleties into them, when their minds are fresh. By the time they have got to the Down clues, some of their subtlety will have been exhausted. They are usually easier.'

John Grant, 1986

Fellow Competitors' Admiration

Whenever John Sykes turned up at the venue for the regional final I was attending, I always felt comfortable being completely thrashed at solving the crosswords by him. He seemed to prove the theory that there were aliens among us.

Don Henderson

THE TIMES OBITUARY: JOHN SYKES

7th September 1993

THE son of a borough treasurer, John Sykes was one of the cleverest men of his generation. His life can be divided into three major segments and one spectacular hobby. Starting out as a theoretical physicist, he became an inspired translator and progressed from there to being an expert lexicographer all the time maintaining his form as the most redoubtable competitor in *The Times* National Crossword Championship.

From St Lawrence College, Ramsgate, John Bradbury Sykes went up to Wadham College, Oxford, to read mathematics, and having taken his first degree, went on to write a DPhil thesis on aspects of theoretical solar physics. In 1953 he moved to the Atomic Energy Research Establishment at Harwell, where he did some work on neutron migration. The authorities soon discovered that his real interest lay in another direction, namely translation. His phenomenal memory enabled him to acquire an outline knowledge of any language remarkably quickly (at the time of his death he had just added Welsh to his collection). The essence of his aptitude was speed: as an undergraduate he once went home for two weeks at Christmas and returned to Oxford able to translate Russian scientific papers.

In 1958 he was appointed head of the translations office at Harwell, a post which he held, to begin with, virtually single-handed. He was required to translate documents of many kinds from several languages, especially German and Russian, but also Spanish, Japanese, and so on.

Around 1970 he discovered a new intellectual challenge. He noticed that the editor of the Supplement to the OED was appealing for earlier printed evidence for a large number of modern words, among which was the astronomical term 'absolute magnitude'. The hunt excited him and he was soon working in the OED department unpaid on Saturday mornings. It was not long before his obvious linguistic skills impressed the Oxford University Press to the extent that he left Harwell to become editor of the *Concise Oxford Dictionary* when the post fell vacant in 1971. This household dictionary had fallen somewhat behind the times but its new navigator brought it back on course, preparing a new sixth edition (published in 1976) with all the inconsistencies removed, the etymologies successfully revised, and the new waves of scientific vocabulary (laser, neutron, and so on) inserted with conspicuous success. He went on to prepare a new edition of *The Pocket Oxford Dictionary* (1978) and a seventh edition of *The Concise Oxford Dictionary* in 1982.

His hobbies were of the kind that one would perhaps expect: chess, bridge, and in a legendary manner the solving of crossword puzzles. When he lived in Abingdon, for example, he used to take the bus to Harwell and had always completed *The Times* Crossword before the bus reached Rowstock Corner, a journey of less than a quarter of an hour. He was the *The Times* National Crossword champion ten times, winning for the last time in 1990 when he solved the four puzzles in an average time of eight minutes each and won by a record margin of nine-and-a-half minutes. (Five years earlier he had resolved to compete only in alternate years in order to give others a chance: had he not made this self-denying ordinance, he would undoubtedly have won even more times.)

Throughout his working life he was renowned for his encyclopaedic grasp of detail, his immense capacity for work and his kindness to colleagues.

THE TIMES CROSSWORD WRECKED

Sir, —Here's one on behalf of the compilers, and my one claim to fame: I'm the only man to wreck the acclaimed *Times* Crossword puzzle.

It would be some 15 years ago when John Grant, the then crossword editor, phoned to say that one of my puzzles would be appearing the following day, Easter Monday.

I duly turned to the back page – and choked on my cornflakes. The clues and the grid did not match! The shame! The ignominy! Fortunately my wife prevented me from cutting my wrists, because later that day John rang to say that it was not my fault – the printers had inserted the wrong grid.

The outcome was interesting. If memory serves me aright John received some 50 letters. Forty were outraged that a paper of the calibre of *The Times* should be guilty of such blatant carelessness; five said they had solved the puzzle anyway by making a grid to fit the clues; and five said, somewhat sarcastically perhaps, what a splendid idea, you should repeat this type of challenge from time to time.

Bob Bartholomew, 2005

FROM THE NINETIES TO 2005

Across

1. Those responsible for split sides but firm middles (9)
6. Scot presented to the Queen is ceremonial officer (5)
9. Master in charge embraces disciple of secret society (7)
10. Manage to draw one side of field (4, 3)
11. Just the tack for a young man! (5)
12. Mineral for an old Russian (9)
14. Note colloidal suspension (3)
15. All help out to make room inside for little Gene (11)
17. Cornet played in church with everyone in alternative building! (7,4)
19. Spoil the planet, emitting sulphur (3)
20. What, at sea, could give brig smear? (9)
22. Maybe a p-painter's screen (5)
24. Diamond territory in this country (7)
26. Fabric obtainable in 'Laura's' (Chelsea) (7)
27. Nick is no companion (5)
28. Sitting in garden in street by a railway (9)

Down

1. Existentialist won't keep quiet in the university (5)
2. Wind and a bit of fog Roman god served up (7)
3. Undervalue squalid habitat with one fireplace (9)
4. One gives better rewards if all the results are right (11)
5. Juice dad's knocked over (3)
6. Second lieutenant has no command of music (5)
7. Community of the Resurrection has willow staff for prelate (7)
8. Sort of educational course making school subject more invigorating (9)
13. Confident like the broker who minds his own business? (4-7)
14. Bigoted believer could make saint care (9)
16. Loamy soil Sonia prepared for carnation (9)
18. Most excellent drama with happy ending (7)
19. Despite what one hears, this drug produces less anxiety (7)
21. Fish—one shouldn't smoke it (5)
23. Army girl to make excursion (5)
25. The Turf getting up entertainments (3)

31 MARCH 1990

HUGE ANTI-POLL TAX DEMONSTRATION CENTRED ON TRAFALGAR SQUARE

Across

1. Fussy individual (10)
9. Shut up in winter, naturally (6)
10. Plant and fish study have excellent backing (8)
11. Reveal it upset one of the family (8)
12. Church body (4)
13. Enraptured by the period before spring? (10)
15. It faces the ground (7)
17. A graduate with true potential, though no expert (7)
20. Laundry, to a point, requires capital (10)
21. King taken in by poor poet (4)
23. The leftist full of beans is spurned (8)
25. Holds in high regard (8)
26. A woman's ambition to make a comeback in *M. N. Dream* (6)
27. The two part without hesitation, which is inconvenient (10)

Down

2. Middle Eastern countries' song about a seaman (6)
3. With no ups and downs in the main (8)
4. Overcrowded conditions costing one work (10)
5. A trainee who'll make a sovereign employee (7)
6. A little water runs with difficulty (4)
7. Basic personal treatment (8)
8. Started green, ended otherwise (10)
12. The new theory won't appear remarkable (10)
14. The French chaps board, which is unsatisfactory (10)
16. Foolish person rises to show a travel document (8)
18. Such people live among giants (8)
19. The boss enters only half—he's learning! (7)
22. Some soldiers think this is to liberate (6)
24. Sportsmen turning up in pink here (4)

This was the qualifying puzzle for the 1991 Times Collins Dictionaries Crossword Championship.

17 JANUARY 1991

BUSH ORDERS ALLIES TO BEGIN BOMBING BAGHDAD

Across

1. Ugly surroundings of square where bandits lurk (4-4)
5. Orders to a senior officer if cut off (6)
10. Frenzied Malawi going round in circles—fuel is hard to find (8, 7)
11. Original estate holds right to a court record (7)
12. One of a couple liable to be removed by a keeper (3, 4)
13. Where the highwayman demanded your money? (4-4)
15. Old form of chair lift (5)
18. More mature sample of alcohol derivative (5)
20. Tinker makes a profit, the cunning fellow (8)
23. Repellent old woman holding mass of dough has to move clumsily (7)
25. Camp in small cottage by lake (7)
26. Philanthropy? It's part of a fallible heresy! (15)
27. The currency is not hard (6)
28. Fear to go rambling without this (4-4)

Down

1. Monkey that utters long doleful cries (6)
2. Mysterious Dickensian grabbing one-foot-wide bit of timber (9)
3. It's a bore to lubricate properly (3, 4)
4. The rise and fall of belief (5)
6. Sergeant detailed to turn out gets mad (7)
7. Mediterranean city turned upside down to accommodate single lady (5)
8. Prince has a thing about the Spanish (8)
9. Unfaithfulness of a grown-up on the end of private line (8)
14. Admirer of beauty scoffed about these resorts (8)
16. Make up one's mind to settle (9)
17. An unlikely bet, putting money on ghost being cast out (4, 4)
19. Right country church for a love story (7)
21. Old-fashioned company—one in Coventry (7)
22. He makes deliveries in Anglo-French waters (6)
24. Not rich, keeping a married mistress (5)
25. Start to cram old ship with freight (5)

This tie-breaker puzzle was solved in 12 minutes at the 1992 Bristol regional final of the Times Intercity Crossword Championship.

16 SEPTEMBER 1992

BRITAIN WITHDRAWS FROM E.R.M.

Across

1. Yob, for example, will approve of non-U language (4, 5)
6. Sulks, having disease (5)
9. Separate from Anglo-Saxon subordinate (7)
10. Urged on to travel for experience (7)
11. Start to sell fruit, and some asparagus (5)
12. Breathe in, out, but don't wake up (9)
13. A local politician has eccentric attire (8)
15. Fail to take tin-opener, so eat less (4)
19. Trollope's Lily of the valley? (4)
20. Bird in summer diving in the river (8)
23. Chant after Julian (9)
24. Tribesmen's qualifications excellent (5)
26. Cumberland tradesman (7)
27. Some fear a chess problem may give a pain in the head (7)
28. Prior or Presbyter (5)
29. Percentage made from connections in high places? (9)

Down

1. Players never asked to take a bow? (5, 4)
2. Heard fire—it drops a man (5)
3. Roman bathhouse had to shut out Veronica (8)
4. An annual payment for this land? (8)
5. Unclean food to hand (6)
6. New way to join the Navy (6)
7. Fat horse, fed with poor grain (9)
8. Addressed the bar (5)
14. Called for calm (9)
16. Delay, so movie star eats in (9)
17. Risk transportation from court (8)
18. Consolation over exam that may be over one's head (8)
21. Protect Shakespeare's Fairy Queen (6)
22. Glass-paper (6)
23. Half hearted, unintelligible words from actor (5)
25. Black Sea resort, so absurdly pretty? Not half! (5)

2 JANUARY 1993

WARRING FACTIONS DISCUSS PEACE FOR BOSNIA

Across

1. About to rise, Henry makes a bloomer (8)
5. Tree that's vulgar, not posh (6)
8. Satisfactory pass, yet at first express dissatisfaction (7-3)
9. A capital ramble, by the sound of it (4)
10. Counterpart to 'pope' is, strangely, 'pop' (8, 6)
11. Play with extremely smart theologian taken in by a trick (7)
13. Piece of business holding the attention (7)
15. Bird pushing stuff (7)
18. Cut and ran, having imbibed a small drink (7)
21. Plant into which James Hogg put his money? (9, 5)
22. Tense but audible, gave instruction (4)
23. From Bombay, a collection of papers one behind another (6, 4)
24. Goddess supplying just part of what he needed (6)
25. Horse in the ark a cob, perhaps (8)

Down

1. Quickly and frequently turned up within call (7)
2. Furtively creep into party (9)
3. Blissful, without being retired (7)
4. Still wearing former set of clothes (7)
5. Plenty in favour of union (9)
6. Soft and suitable for digging, that's the story (7)
7. A suitor could become married (7)
12. When to feed and cultivate, mulch and tine (5-4)
14. Unkind remark like Xerxes, for instance, uttered (9)
16. Arriviste puts a fresh interpretation on pictures (7)
17. Engineers follow their leader into the more remote scene of operations (7)
18. Mum, about to say more, is somewhat mournful (7)
19. Mischievous child destroys looms (7)
20. Least shallow river has a bore (7)

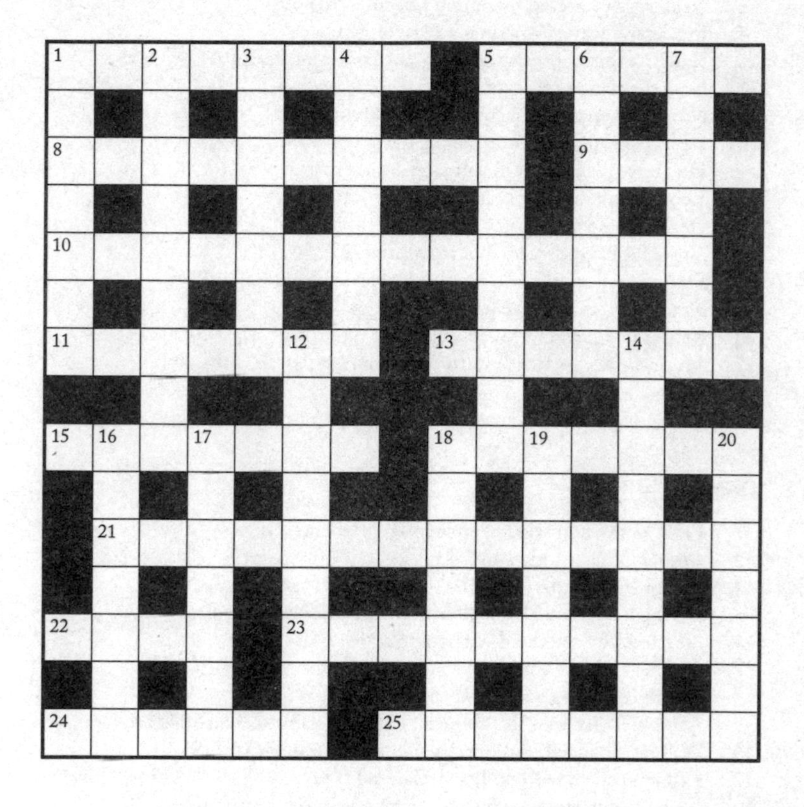

6 MAY 1994

CHANNEL TUNNEL OPENS

Across

1. Neat bedsit rejected by retired salesman (6)
4. Impressive way of agreeing a bargain (8)
10. Rail link for foodstuffs crossing the centre of Paris (9)
11. Nobody's boy, almost wolfish (5)
12. North American policeman's second release (7)
13. Latin poet retracted note about marriage (7)
14. He's turned an insignificant sum into a fortune (5)
15. Loud drunk in front of aircraft? Get knotted! (8)
18. Descend into anticlimax (8)
20. Appallingly cruel source of corruption (5)
23. Perfume once produced for the audience in a theatre (7)
25. Newly-wed in obscure part of America (7)
26. Refuse found round many a city (5)
27. Music-maker no one backed after concert (9)
28. Charge includes the replacement of nose ring (8)
29. Summons served by governor makes us squirm (6)

Down

1. Party workers divided about record of events (8)
2. Throw into confusion by taking boat across river (7)
3. Volatile former partner with message about appeal (9)
5. In which energetic behaviour may be discussed with heat (14)
6. He's too lazy to take the wheel (5)
7. Driving force of a mischief-maker in France and America (7)
8. Not rough though in a bait (6)
9. Absorb choice role and respond with cheerful tolerance (4,2,4,4)
16. Will his financial impropriety come out in the wash? (9)
17. Fashion centre with no floral material? (8)
19. Lacking equipment—but we won't get into a row! (7)
21. He appears in about six books identifying sheep (7)
22. Southern athlete with a friendly expression (6)
24. Republican thus involved in an act of criminal destruction (5)

This puzzle was solved within 30 minutes by 24 per cent of the competitors at the York regional final of the Times Crossword Championship.

19 APRIL 1995

MANY FEARED DEAD IN OKLAHOMA BOMBING

Across

1. Go over the plot—I'm hard to please (10)
6. Some columns, to Athenians (4)
10. Use an airline in the process of expansion? (7)
11. Deny ringing women's prison (7)
12. Harmful effect of cold—best for it to be treated (9)
13. Bound to be embarrassed about shortage of work? (5)
14. Fruit of tree—a trick to snare first of race? (5)
15. Silly moment, getting rid of first new hired help (9)
17. US writer making money here on book (4,5)
20. Gulls may be caught the day it begins (5)
21. Put together a written text when imprisoned (5)
23. Loutish one abroad appears to annoy worker (9)
25. Damn pet disappeared! (7)
26. Wire had damaged some leather (7)
27. Penniless person keen on culture (4)
28. Went over again, to secure once more backing in special trade (10)

Down

1. This chap's on Ben's side, possibly (5)
2. Sick of company tucking into meal? (3,6)
3. Don't run off before hearing its report (8,6)
4. A graduate goes around Viking territory overseas (7)
5. Offer admission for a charge (7)
7. Traditional outdoor type of carriage parking (5)
8. Relying on hearsay can lead to error (9)
9. Circus performer the second person retracting? (5-9)
14. A very old port I got out for the 'The Queen' (9)
16. American who knows the ropes ties a liar in knots (9)
18. Instrument from this country you said the French replicated (7)
19. Pursue revolutionary, making brisk progress (7)
22. Special language skill? Try to crack it (5)
24. Director at first supports sentimental material (5)

28 AUGUST 1996

DIVORCE BETWEEN
PRINCE CHARLES AND PRINCESS
DIANA IS FINALIZED

Across

1. Like a group of people surrounding a French court (8)
6. Busy tenant (6)
9. Support part of orchestra's recovery (6, 4)
10. Memory associated with piano concert (4)
11. Arrangement that results in falling sales (5, 7)
13. The last author one would expect to find in the Index? (4)
14. Where tracks are made available to the public (2, 6)
17. It can provide work regularly in post (4, 4)
18. King likely to get carried away (4)
20. Material girl needed to make pancake (5, 7)
23. Market square (4)
24. A part of speech hidden by mysterious singer (6-4)
25. One likely to succeed in the long run? (6)
26. Open to wind, but protected from rain—anything in it? (8)

Down

2. Deplored initial version of game given by journalist (4)
3. After family row, vital assets are stored here (5, 4)
4. Untidy mess overlooked by gardener originally (6)
5. Left crew working with flier in this English town (8, 7)
6. Conservative group getting on with police (3, 5)
7. Changing topic, get into trouble (3, 2)
8. What's still to be seen after it's been taken? (10)
12. Unlikely to run and pass our fleet (6–4)
15. Luggage from vehicle Paddy appears to steal (6–3)
16. Social conflict as pupils turned up unprepared (5, 3)
19. Goddess from heathen antiquity (6)
21. Composer's block (5)
22. Legal document showing right, in some sense (4)

2 MAY 1997

LABOUR ROUTS TORIES IN HISTORIC ELECTION

Across

1. Returned copies containing a single drawing (5)
4. Protection for members getting lots of letters asking for money? (5-4)
9. Happy colleague with right frame of mind (9)
10. Ventilated anger in newspaper item (5)
11. Stamp or step on it (3,4,4,4)
12. Sort of safe seat in which high-flier may survive (7)
14. Mostly grand style not unknown in work of James, for example (7)
16. Stir drink while eating fish (5,2)
19. Pinafore's original producer (3-4)
21. Boy and girl carrying mother's plant (10,5)
23. Peel's hound runs more unswervingly (5)
24. Staff provided points to appear in policy statement (9)
25. Like Roman emperors, for example, not popular (9)
26. Instrument unknown in piping (5)

Down

1. Fudge to pack in cupboard (4,5)
2. A fluid mover just beat the favourite, we hear (7)
3. This stage is a month ahead (5)
4. Warship's weight (7)
5. Expert admitting educational establishment is solvent (7)
6. Vixen finally going to ground in narrow escape (4,5)
7. Publicise harbour where many travellers land (7)
8. Study at US city, having taken things on board (5)
13. Its owner should never be lost for words (9)
15. Each one by end of game is extremely stiff (9)
17. Plant producing ash can start to upset constituents (7)
18. Compile material for controversial discussion (7)
19. Use soft soap for this fabric (7)
20. New edition of book about children (7)
21. Old Greek alien getting only 50% in arithmetic (5)
22. Submit notes in succession to the king (5)

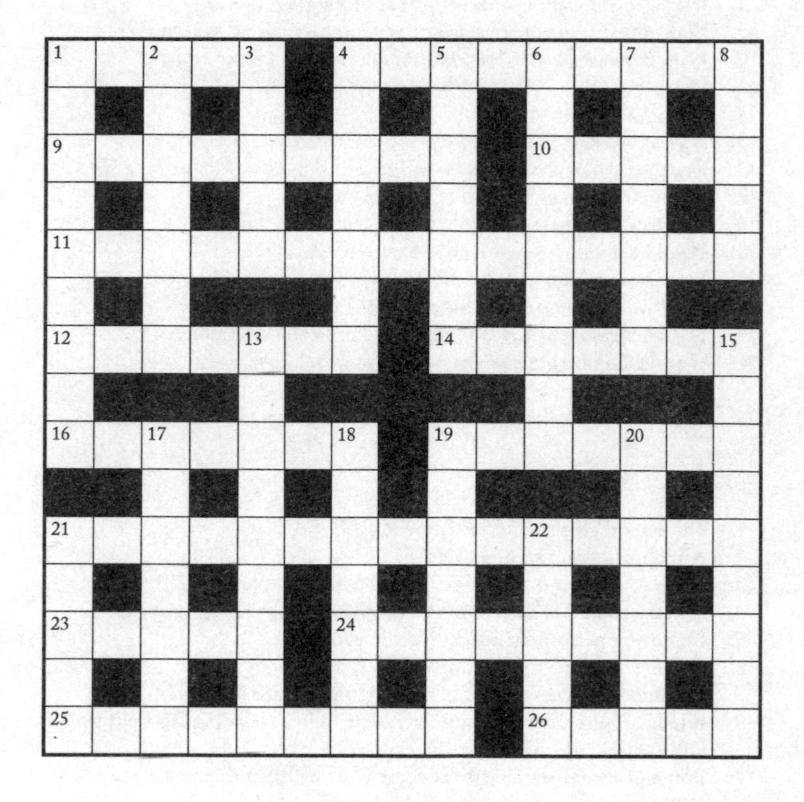

10 APRIL 1998

GOOD FRIDAY AGREEMENT IS REACHED IN NORTHERN IRELAND

Across

1. It could spoil what's programmed for tomorrow (10,3)
9. Way reverse of fortune on board produces decisive situations (9)
10. Britons of the first millennium taking rocks to part of Ireland (5)
11. Hard to get into restaurant commonly? Nonsense! (5)
12. Man of the millennium? (4)
13. Aim to depart before 3.15 (4)
15. Beginner who's paid a pound? (7)
17. Classic that makes English racing special (7)
18. Distinctions—several hundreds of them in 2000 (7)
20. People as found, note, round centre of Ghana (7)
21. Female undergarment you might spot in millenium (4)
22. In 2000, English band of little note (4)
23. Group of colonists fighting in second millenium, originally (5)
26. 'e meets Lambeth girl, or one from Lissom Grove (5)
27. Dance in social I organised (9)
28. What will mark the start of the new millennium? Exactly! (9,4)

Down

1. Show good girls an old instrument (7,7)
2. A Christmassy chap upset her (5)
3. Distress and fear one may get tonight, for example (3,2,2,3)
4. It's very close, not far across the river (3,4)
5. Improving performance in cups, win games (7)
6. Give instructions to cut cheese (4)
7. Like modern arrangement of dates, with a choice of boys (9)
8. Building done with minimum chaos, with lines heading East put in? (10,4)
14. Bottle of wine—he bought it some years before reaching millennium (10)
16. Setting about very long fish (9)
19. Instruction not to correct boy under head's protection (7)
20. A resting-place I provided for South American rodent (7)
24. One's covered by Jack and Bill—you can count on them (5)
25. Composer from start of Christian era (4)

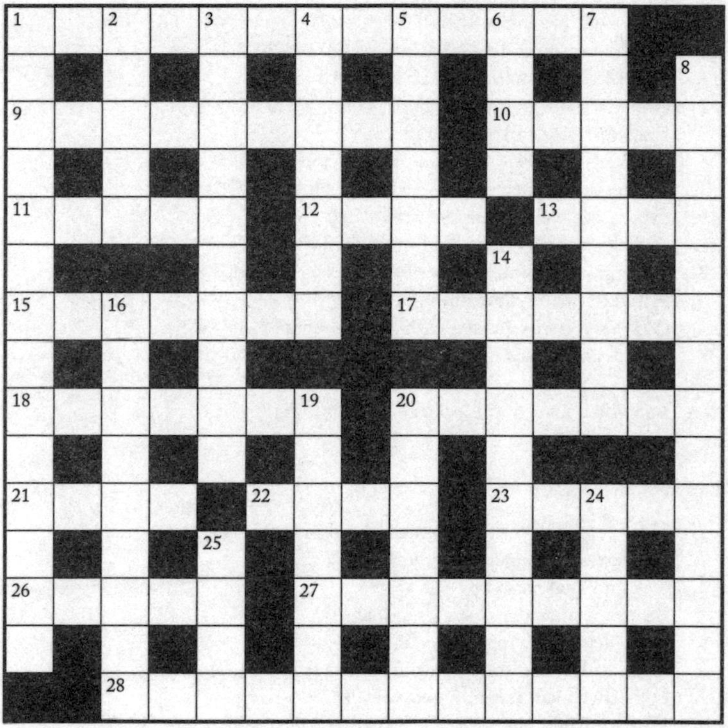

31 DECEMBER 1999

PUTIN TAKES OVER AS YELTSIN RESIGNS

Across

1. Old-fashioned writing in work repelled actor (5)
4. One goes over the top in battle (9)
9. Divert out of harbour (9)
10. Turn to big noise to get backing (5)
11. Capital city, as announced in sequence (6)
12. Noble act represented in operatic style (3,5)
14. Encounters one playing in attack (9)
16. Old king or queen, for example, rejected deadly lawmaker (5)
17. Publication turned round—editor took risks (5)
19. Principal musical composition for top band (9)
21. Security system's tight hold on university (4,4)
22. Bookmaker's work, in theory—selecting the odds (6)
25. Fish, after short time, biting at lake (5)
26. Old piano part repeated without one note? Fine! (4-5)
27. What can provide light entertainment? This sort of contest, of course (5,4)
28. Individual investing Eastern capital in Asia (5)

Down

1. How people in theatre work essential programs (9,6)
2. Request for lift, so pull up with a jerk (5)
3. Jack and I taken in by Silas (7)
4. Bishop is moved across a diagonal (4)
5. Facial feature giving rise to light gossip? (7,3)
6. Head of Eastern state—top Oriental fellow (4,3)
7. Full-length van taken by seducer (9)
8. Distinguished observer of unusually early star or moon (10,5)
13. Stinking fish found in educational establishment (4,6)
15. Readily accepting protest after one gets minimal raise (9)
18. Femme fatale cheered up when line accepted (7)
20. Serve in special force that protects the rear (7)
23. From old Asian capital, shift to its modern counterpart (5)
24. Bank short of a pound—really! (4)

4 AUGUST 2000

QUEEN MOTHÈR CELEBRATES CENTENARY

Across

1. Revealing certain statistics that may have been inflated? (4,5)
6. Obliquely referring to botanic gardens (5)
9. New nurse making marks on old tablets (5)
10. Stock control impossible during such rushes (9)
11. Distemper flat needed put on with difficulty (4,3)
12. Distinct community in French grotto, about fifty (7)
13. Has responsibility for carriages showing symbols of military rank (8-6)
17. Quartet play this commission by English composer (8,6)
21. His responsibility still remains to be seen (7)
23. Footplate, perhaps, provided elation when in motion (7)
25. Sort of roll, A–E etc? (9)
26. Money one might charge in Africa (5)
27. To eat sparingly makes sense (5)
28. Great bed depository? (9)

Down

1. Shop successfully, given some leverage (8)
2. Person in Greece, a hopeless case (5)
3. Cricket guide—one examining details of flight, spin, etc (4,5)
4. Live outside university for the rest (7)
5. In sale, men found fashionable hard-wearing coats (7)
6. Savoury relish—a flavouring using shortening? (5)
7. Leather finally selected for backing novel (9)
8. Hardy characters lived there (6)
14. Uses old or new type of method to defeat sniffer-dogs (9)
15. Element thin on the ground? (4,5)
16. Spring socially acceptable for expression of praise (4,4)
18. Team up? (7)
19. See such a bishop has given old name (7)
20. Stress feature of dialect? (6)
22. It goes up on the tenth (5)
24. Go out dressed in gold for so long (5)

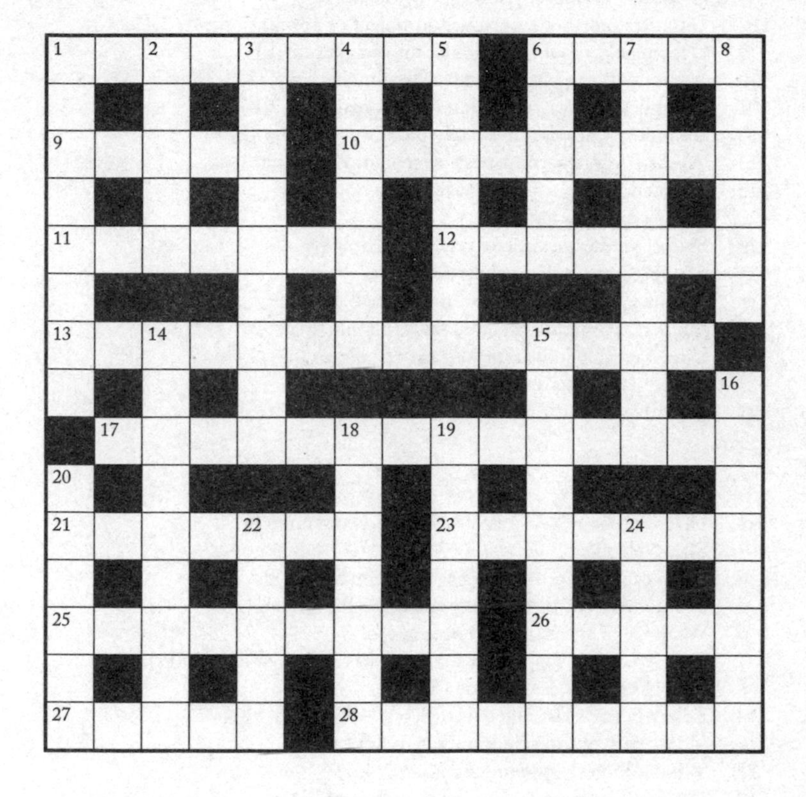

21 FEBRUARY 2001

BAN FOLLOWS FOOT-AND-MOUTH OUTBREAK

Across

1. Depression caused by shortage of drink (3, 7)
7. One firm, northern, becomes an object of admiration (4)
9. Dependable about being under an obligation? (8)
10. Barrier put up right from the start for the sick (6)
11. Complicated laws restricting the Spanish too (2, 4)
12. Completely despise ultimately bloodthirsty story (8)
13. Woman's given second-best ingredient for recipe? (4)
15. Exposed lover—could it have led to hot water? (5, 5)
18. Clearly aren't in use (10)
20. Part of garment could be yellow, we hear (4)
21. Support worker that's shot? (8)
24. No time for nurse's work—that's final! (6)
26. Jumped up, getting the latest information, and phoned (6)
27. Unfashionable jobs in far distant territories (8)
28. Sound battery to dispose of (4)
29. Stormy scenes at the RSC (3, 7)

Down

2. Deliveries bound, we're told, to start being late? (9)
3. Slap Nick (5)
4. Main cable broken causing a lack of stability (9)
5. Diamonds—cards that may be of use for a flush (3, 4)
6. Wrap tip of specially hard boring tool (5)
7. One left, given support by comrade in a criminal manner (9)
8. One has shown error inside (5)
14. Reject Potter's last objective (9)
16. Noon, perhaps, in senior citizens' club (3, 6)
17. What a forger's apprentice may do (4, 5)
19. Put small amount on European swimmer (7)
22. Current measure getting on top of the French Liberal (5)
23. Unusual stag night at first, feeling worried? (5)
25. Fall in love? On the contrary, wilt (5)

14 JANUARY 2002

UK DECLARED FREE OF FOOT-AND-MOUTH

Across

1. The girl got married, exhibited in bygone style (6)
5. A lady must include plot in novel (4,4)
9. Man perhaps trailing vehicle that's left city (8)
10. A son given shelter and softly slumbering (6)
11. Stick to ring road to find town (8)
12. Opening a hut is tricky (6)
13. Women initially hurry having cigarette in dockside accommodation (8)
15. Test gold against common metal (4)
17. Half of the dissidents present (4)
19. Charge man too much for fish (8)
20. See some of the French weep (6)
21. Feudal lord one found in far-flung regions (8)
22. Former US President not completely faithful chap (6)
23. Doing nothing in first part of performance having very little energy (8)
24. The fellow to squat by goddess and dither (8)
25. Enthusiastic call from people losing head and heart (6)

Down

2. Listen to row becoming more energetic (8)
3. Wolf maybe providing sport for guns? (8)
4. Interrupted by one's boy, poet almost sounding harsh (9)
5. A contemporaneous boss seen to be progressive (5,2,4,4)
6. Letter I have written in support of girl (7)
7. Do fish when it starts to get dark (8)
8. Exhibition certain to get publicity (8)
14. A regiment trained to shoot (9)
15. Wife's venerable language (3,5)
16. Everybody can name this Oxford college (3,5)
17. Wriggly python, one cold and bewitching (8)
18. One goes round, needed for a roulette game? (8)
19. Worker upset about vehicle blocking street (7)

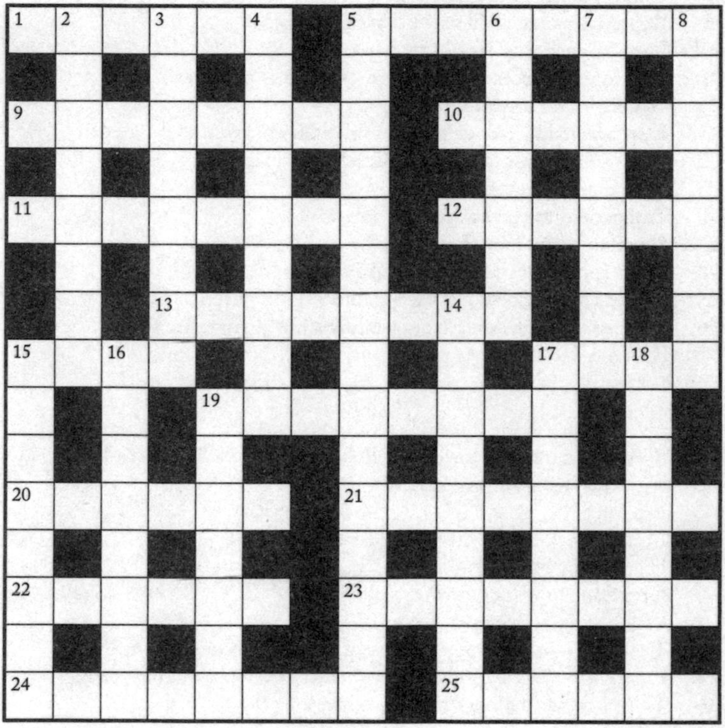

1 JANUARY 2003

EURO HITS STREETS OF 15 COUNTRIES

Across

1. Having attempted a tackle, has got wiped out (4,3,1,6)
9. Orange, brown, and green I mixed (9)
10. Ill-bred person couldn't at first give a toss (5)
11. Firm hampered by lack of money (5)
12. Offer one's services in adaptation of novel—true? (9)
13. Game bird returned to new home (8)
15. Fruit rejected by lad with exceptional talent (6)
17. What brings grist to the mill? Cricket, perhaps (6)
19. Fully extended, eventually (2,6)
22. Cathedral that's bizarre and remote (5,4)
23. Some unceremonious language (5)
24. Man's spoken of busy junction (5)
25. Bombardment finally creates inferno (9)
26. I had to succumb when embraced by a lively, attractive woman (1,3,2,3,5)

Down

1. Receiving a tracheotomy, you will be reprimanded (3,2,2,3,4)
2. Figure twelve worn by horse (7)
3. Fast boats (5)
4. Recreate means of controlling opening (8)
5. Hang over game (6)
6. Direct one to work out what's obscure (9)
7. Rich having no let-up at work (7)
8. The French upset familiar Prussian king and Saxon one (6,3,5)
14. Paper's head journalist at centre of current exemplary court case (9)
16. This place, with others around, is heavenly (8)
18. Take lead going round different plant (7)
20. Dazzling girl's outside with a token of affection (7)
21. Mountain centre with service provided (6)
23. Plane sheltering fifty from the sun (5)

11 MARCH 2004

MADRID TERRORIST ATTACK ON TRAINS

Across

1. Not natural to be attacked (8)
5. Keep carrying box (6)
10. Colour part of eye with end of crayon (5)
11. Always 50% off, in transport plan (9)
12. Career lay in ruins: having started, one couldn't finish it (5, 4)
13. Ulysses was Greek, a soldier (5)
14. A witticism cracked by teacher about Ovid, for one (7)
16. Period in which ideology brings consternation (6)
19. Relent and think about honours (6)
21. Is leading each swell of opposition (4, 3)
23. Match with a foreigner broken off (5)
25. Back what Guardian does? (9)
27. Not like lamb's lettuce stuffed into stomachs endlessly (9)
28. House team (5)
29. Succeeded during term of office? This caller thinks not (6)
30. Measures of protection from talons: substance of nail commonly sheathed (4, 4)

Down

1. Wave that surges through sea, found in branches (8)
2. Without responsibilities or solid means of support? (4–5)
3. Shrewd move of Nancy's (5)
4. Well-turned short poem, essential Dante (7)
6. Painstaking medical procedure? (9)
7. Army picking a conscript up in the Russian zone (5)
8. Quantity the Romans had in excess? (6)
9. Fail to get out saw (6)
15. In Jim Hawkins' father's line, some name-dropping is appropriate (2, 7)
17. Country, in short, is wizard! (9)
18. Arranges each is to leave prison (8)
20. Pinched new weapon (6)
21. Broke toe—have to stop (5,2)
22. At last, traffic light may appear on road (6)
24. Game Boy instructions (5)
26. Like the Web? Ladies have a change of heart (5)

31 OCTOBER 2005

2005 ANNIVERSARY PUZZLE

TIMES CROSSWORD EDITORS

Ronald Carton	*February 1930 – July 1960*
Jane Carton	*July 1960 – September 1965*
Edmund Akenhead	*September 1965 – September 1983*
John Grant	*October 1983 – October 1995*
Brian Greer	*October 1995 – August 2000*
Mike Laws	*August 2000 – September 2002*
Richard Browne	*September 2002 – current*

SOLUTIONS

1 FEBRUARY 1930 *p. 23*

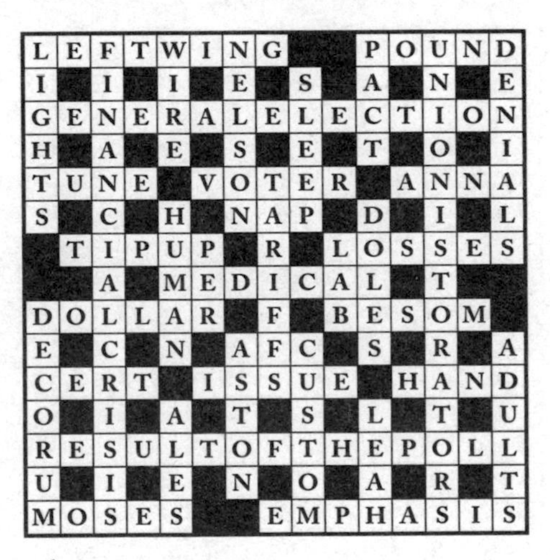

26 OCTOBER 1931 *p. 25*

14 APRIL 1932 *p. 27*

14 OCTOBER 1933 *p. 29*

6 JULY 1934 *p.31*

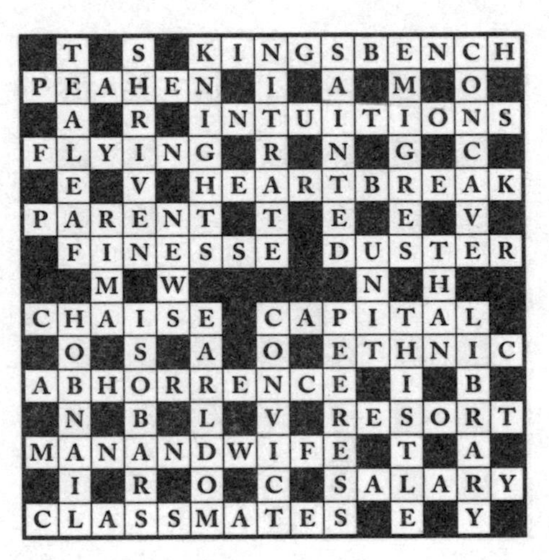

16 MARCH 1935 *p.33*

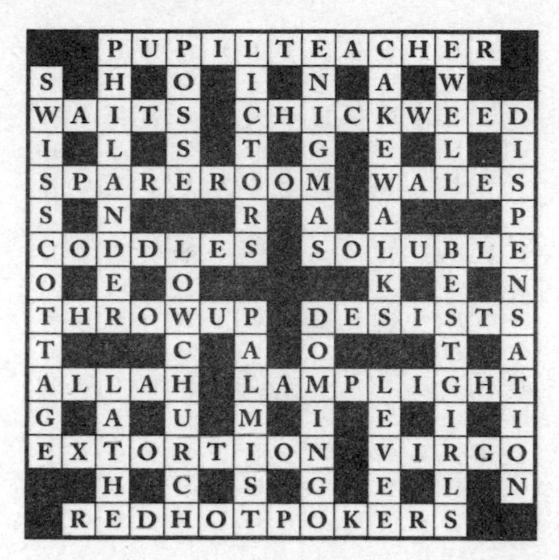

11 DECEMBER 1936 *p.35*

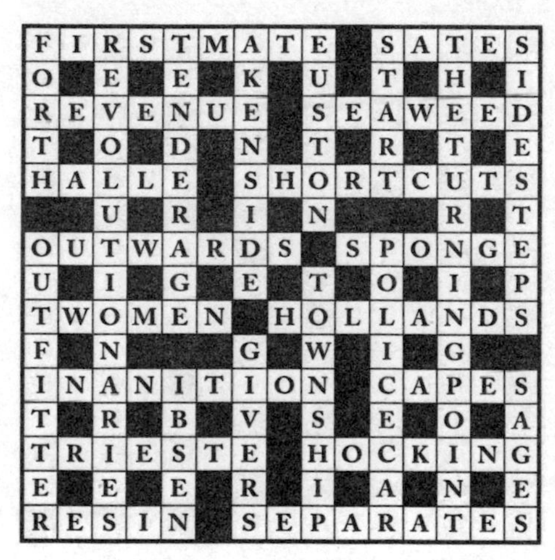

28 MAY 1937 *p.37*

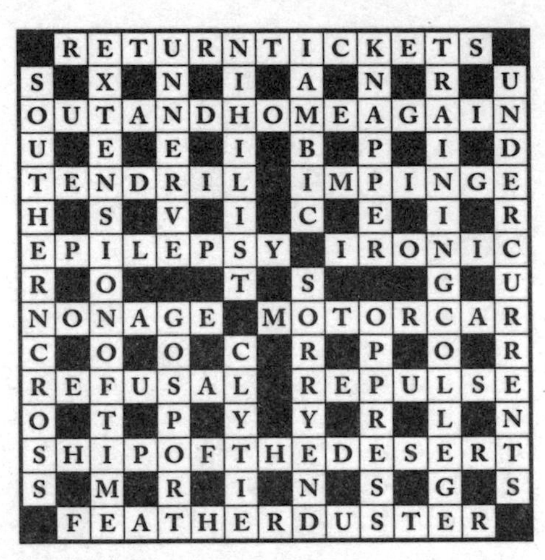

29 SEPTEMBER 1938 *p.39*

1 SEPTEMBER 1939 *p. 41*

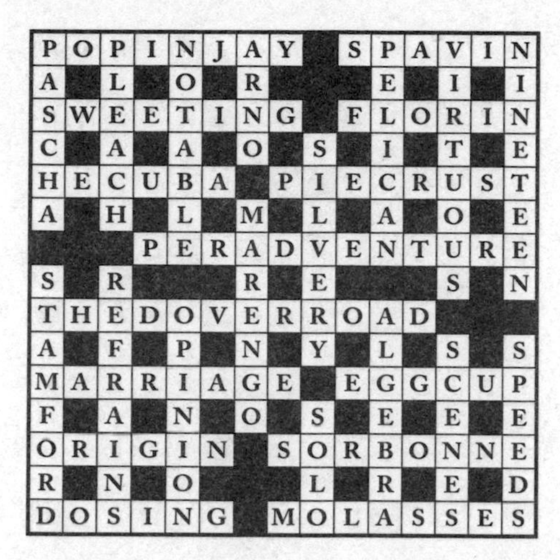

21 AUGUST 1940 *p. 51*

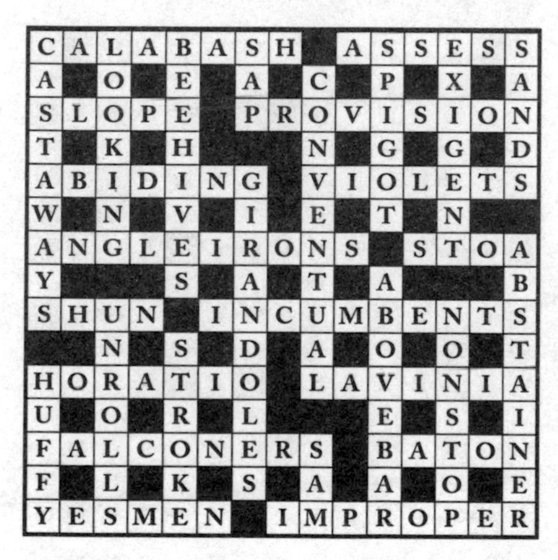

11 DECEMBER 1941 *p. 53*

1 JANUARY 1942 *p.* 55

2 FEBRUARY 1943 *p.* 57

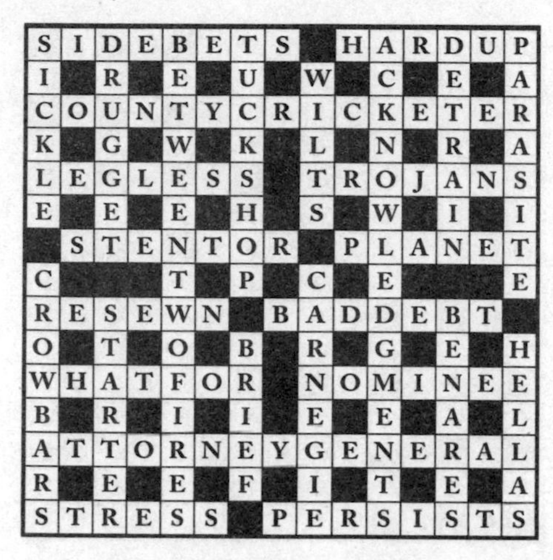

27 JANUARY 1944 *p. 59*

1 MAY 1945 *p. 61*

5 MARCH 1946 *p. 63*

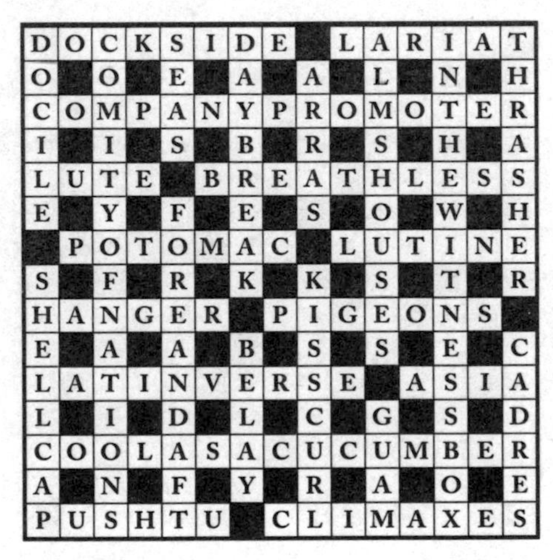

15 AUGUST 1947 *p. 65*

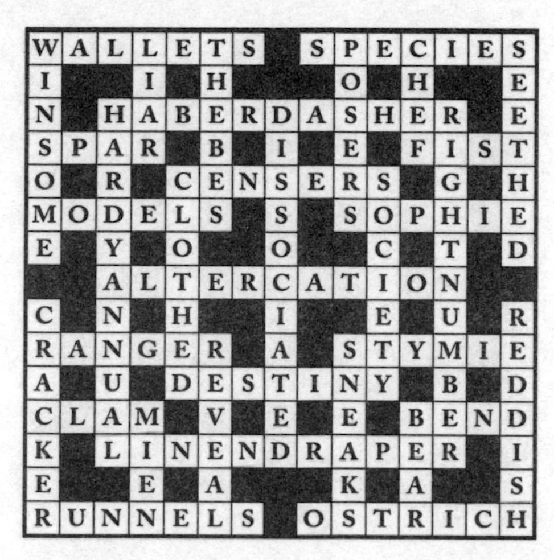

14 MAY 1948 *p. 67*

4 APRIL 1949 *p. 69*

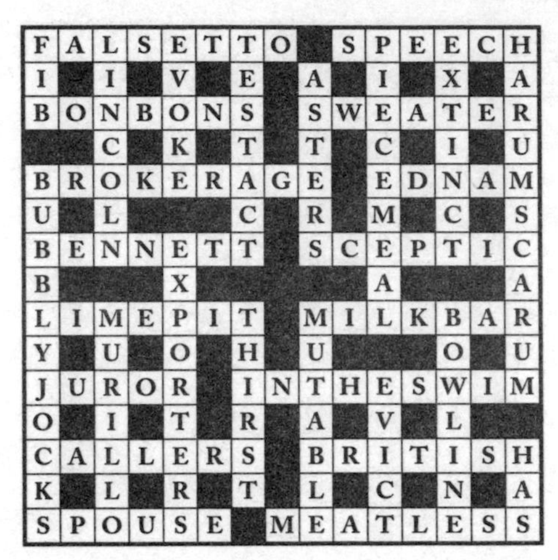

21 JANUARY 1950 *p.81*

26 OCTOBER 1951 *p.83*

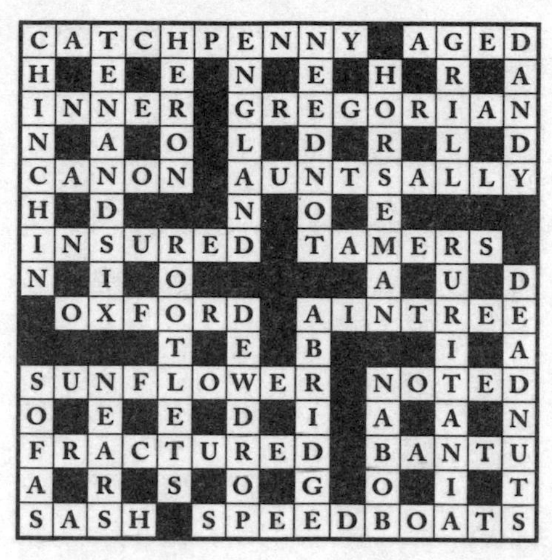

7 JULY 1952 *p. 85*

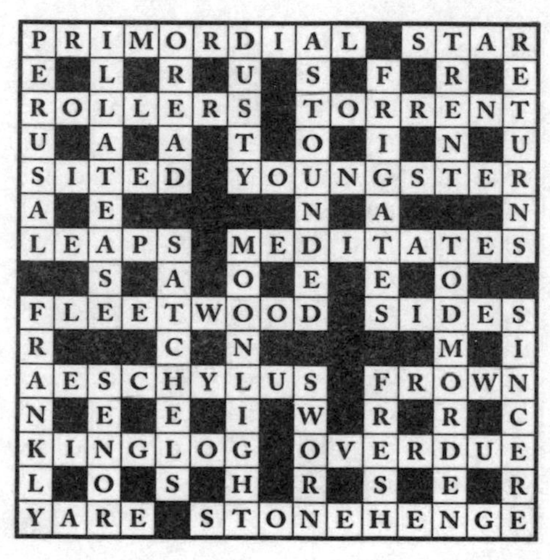

29 MAY 1953 *p. 87*

3 APRIL 1954 *p. 89*

9 MAY 1955 *p. 91*

26 JULY 1956 *p. 93*

10 JANUARY 1957 *p. 95*

4 JANUARY 1958 *p. 97*

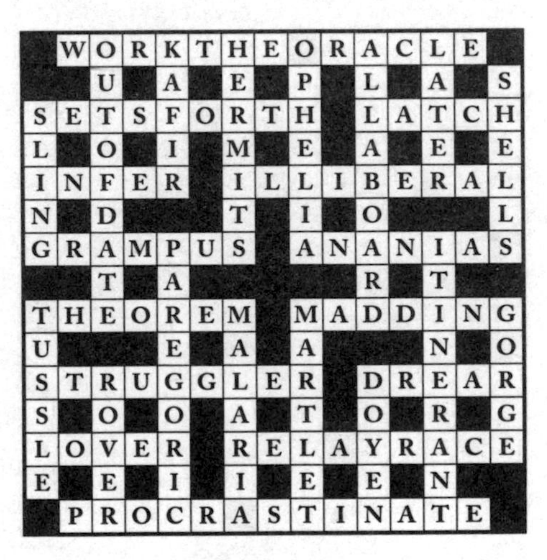

1 JANUARY 1959 *p. 99*

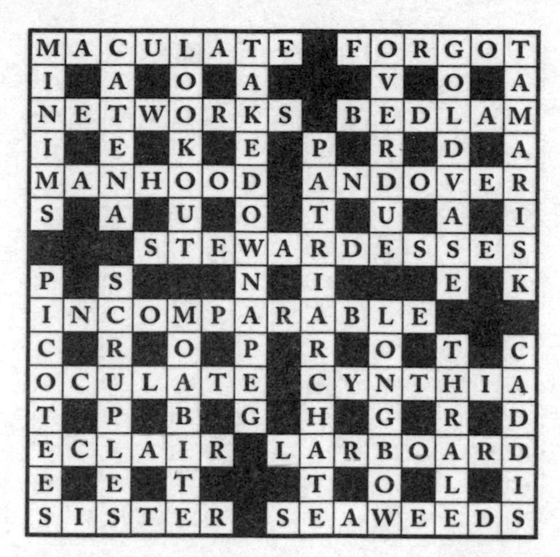

20 JULY 1960 *p. 107*

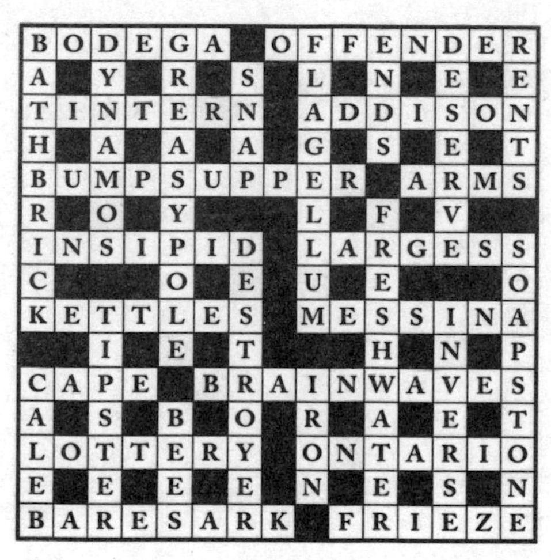

20 JANUARY 1961 *p. 109*

26 APRIL 1962 *p. 111*

14 JANUARY 1963 *p. 113*

12 JUNE 1964 *p. 115*

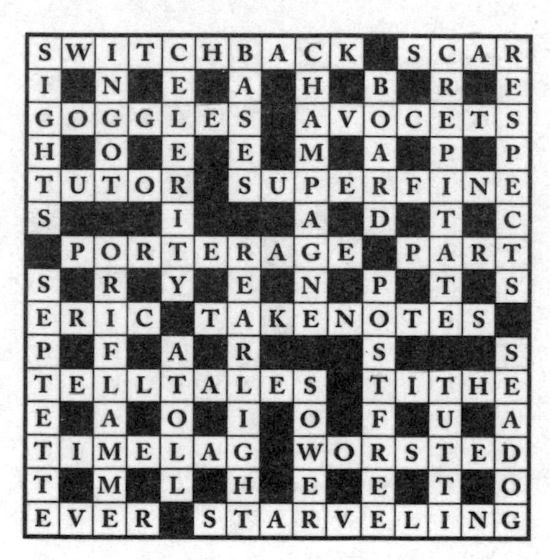

18 JUNE 1965 *p. 117*

20 OCTOBER 1966 *p. 119*

5 JUNE 1967 *p. 121*

4 APRIL 1968 *p. 123*

21 JULY 1969 *p. 125*

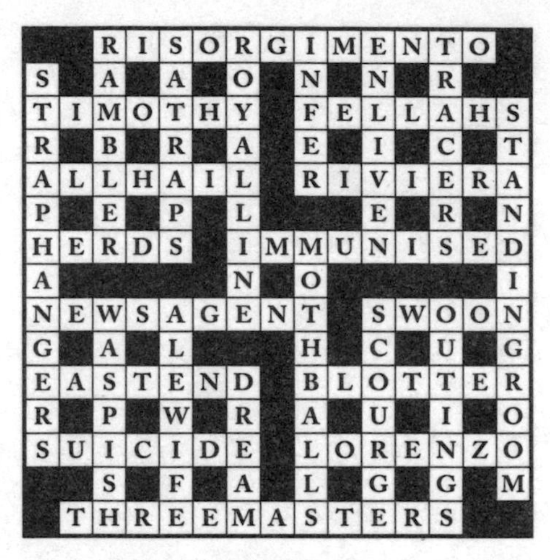

22 JANUARY 1970 *p. 129*

9 AUGUST 1971 *p. 131*

16 FEBRUARY 1972 *p. 133*

26 MARCH 1973 *p. 135*

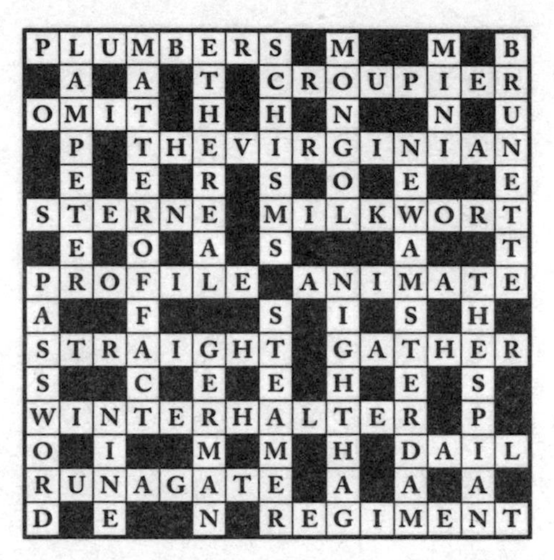

17 JUNE 1974 *p. 137*

9 JUNE 1975 *p. 139*

16 MARCH 1976 *p. 141*

16 AUGUST 1977 *p. 143*

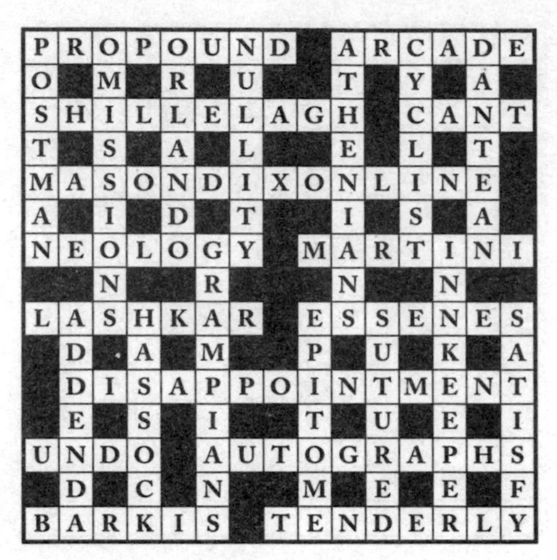

25 JULY 1978 *p. 145*

13 NOVEMBER 1979 *p. 147*

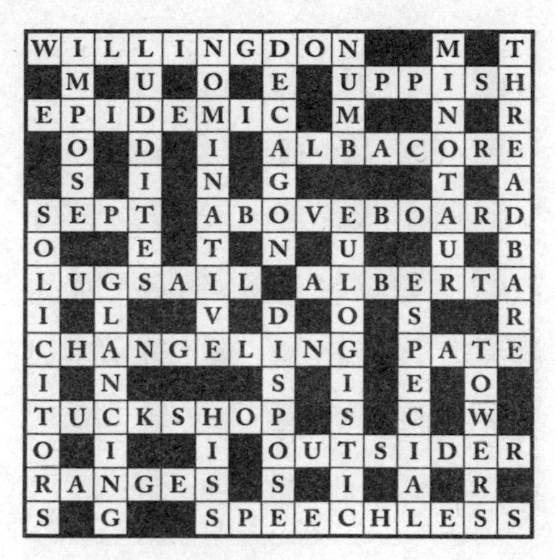

2 JANUARY 1980 *p. 153*

29 JULY 1981 *p. 155*

29 MAY 1982 *p. 157*

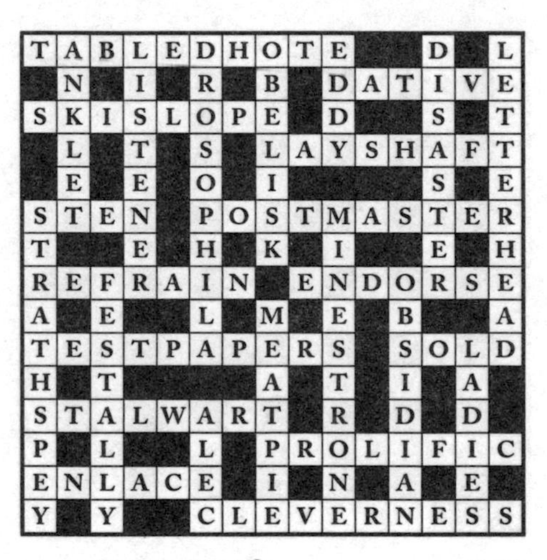

17 JANUARY 1983 *p. 159*

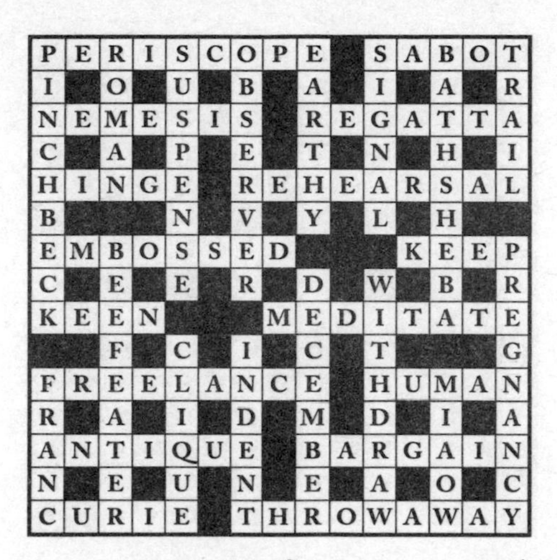

14 FEBRUARY 1984 *p. 161*

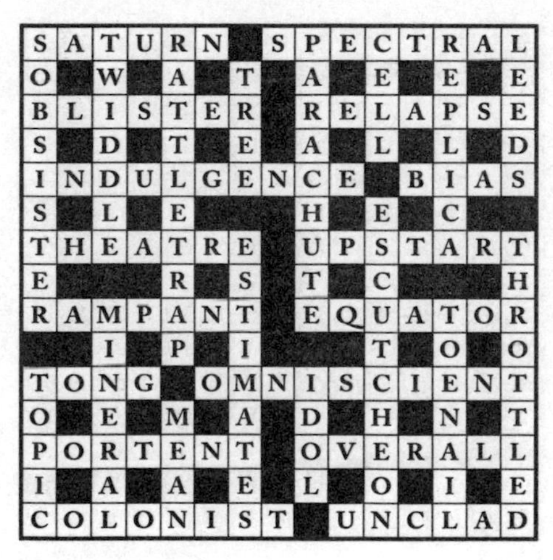

13 JULY 1985 *p. 163*

27 JANUARY 1986 *p. 165*

19 OCTOBER 1987 *p. 167*

3 DECEMBER 1988 *p. 169*

9 NOVEMBER 1989 *p. 171*

31 MARCH 1990 *p. 197*

17 JANUARY 1991 *p. 199*

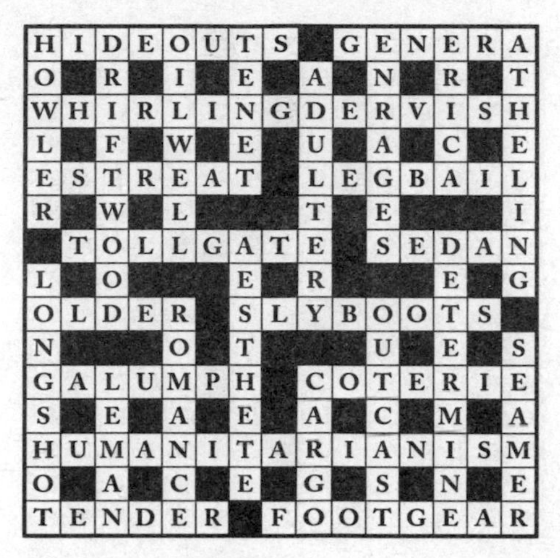

16 SEPTEMBER 1992 *p. 201*

2 JANUARY 1993 *p. 203*

18 MARCH 1993 *p. 11*

Morse — Whodunnit?

Hidden in the grid are the names of
Barrington Pheloung (composer), John Thaw (actor),
and Colin Dexter (creator),
from the Inspector Morse TV series.

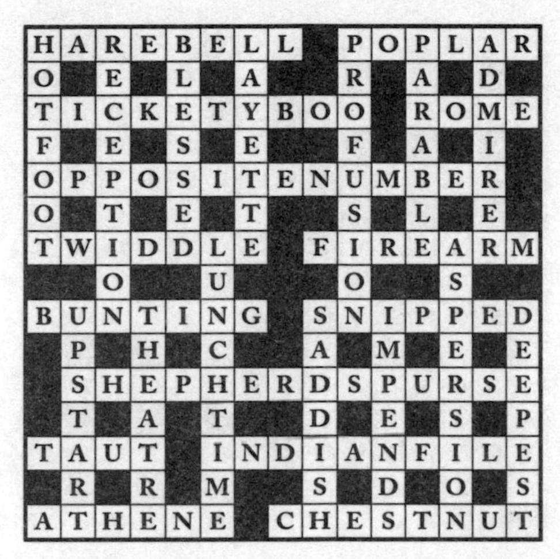

6 MAY 1994 *p. 205*

19 APRIL 1995 *p. 207*

PUZZLE NO.1 *p.177*

1995 Crossword Competition

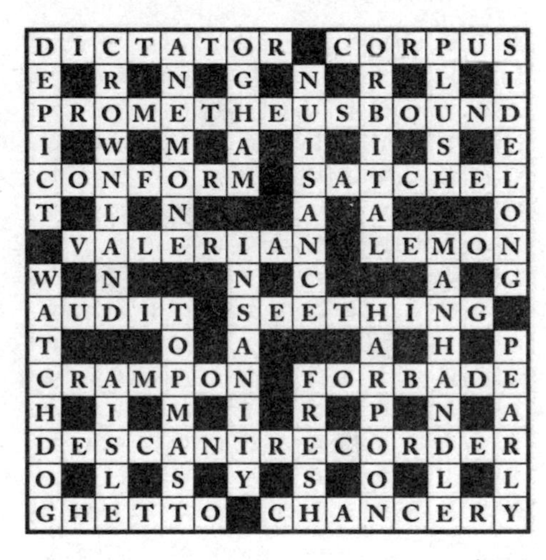

PUZZLE NO.2 *p.179*

1995 Crossword Competition

PUZZLE NO.3 *p. 181*

1995 Crossword Competition

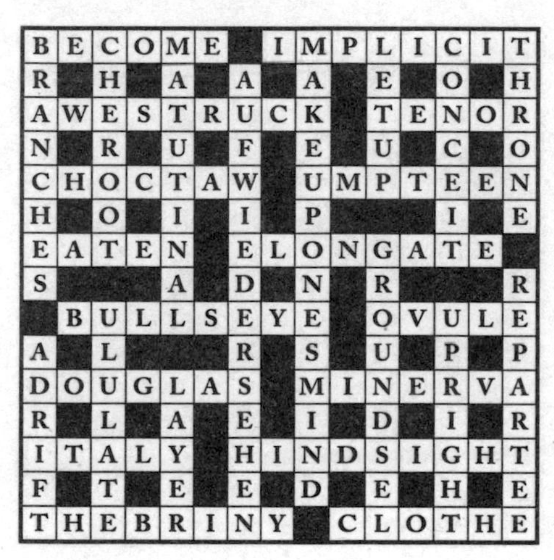

PUZZLE NO.4 *p. 183*

1995 Crossword Competition

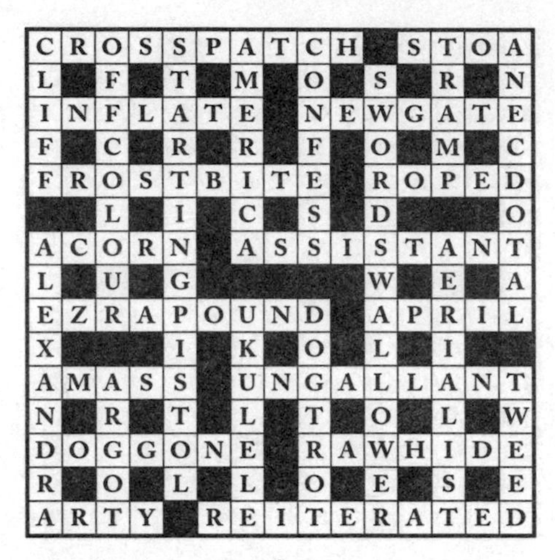

28 AUGUST 1996 *p. 209*

2 MAY 1997 *p. 211*

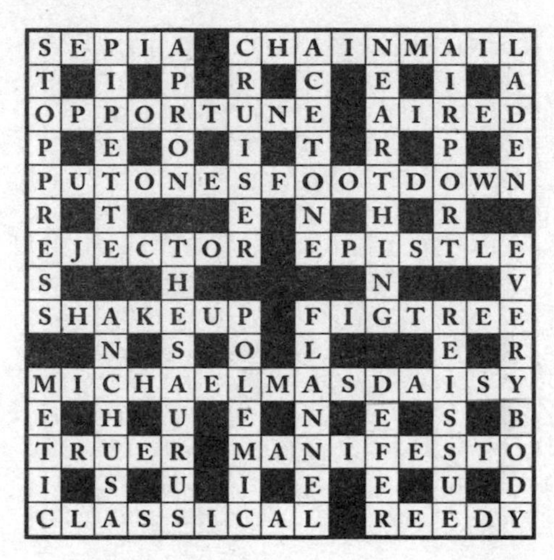

10 APRIL 1998 *p. 213*

31 DECEMBER 1999 *p. 215*

4 AUGUST 2000 *p. 217*

21 FEBRUARY 2001 *p. 219*

14 JANUARY 2002 *p. 221*

1 JANUARY 2003 *p. 223*

11 MARCH 2004 *p. 225*

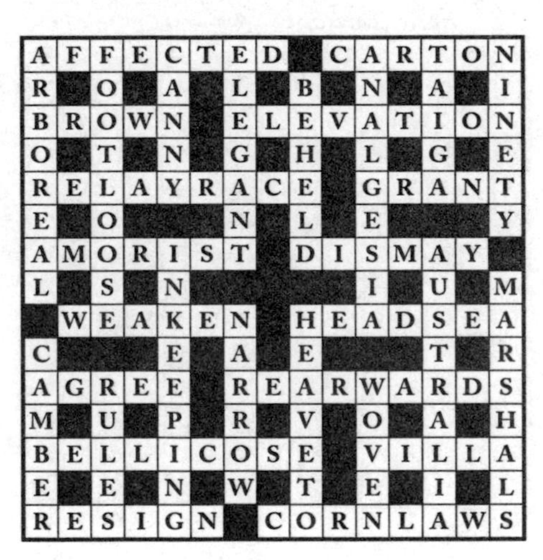

2005 ANNIVERSARY PUZZLE *p. 227*

Solutions for Beerbohm's bogus crossword from 1940 are as follows:

1 *ac*	DISRAELI	1 *dn*	DRAKE'S
23 *ac*	OVERCAME	16 *dn*	HOT CROSS
		19 *dn*	'ARBOUR

The Times' current compilers have various ideas about the sixth clue, but can't agree on any one 'obvious' candidate.

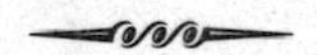

Times Readers' Favourite Clues Solutions for page 70 and 71

1. RHYME
2. DROP OFF
3. ELEMENTS
4. MUSH
5. LANCASTER
6. SNEEZY
7. ETHER
8. SIREN

9. STANDOFFISH

10. BUDDHISM

11. TACITUS

12. EXIST

13. BARDOLATRY

14. SECOND IN COMMAND

15. ONE FINE DAY

16. AGONY AUNT

17. PETER PAN

18. MR RIGHT

19. SPACE BAR

20. BEER BELLY

21. SCANTIES

22. ARARAT

23. CLOUDLESS

24. DANDELION CLOCK

25. MISAPPROPRIATES

26. RUN DOWN

27. HECATOMBS